AN OTHER DAY AN OTHER TIME

GOLDWYN MILLS

authorHOUSE

AuthorHouse™
1663 Liberty Drive
Bloomington, IN 47403
www.authorhouse.com
Phone: 1 (800) 839-8640

Published by AuthorHouse 03/31/2020

ISBN: 978-1-7283-5064-6 (sc)
ISBN: 978-1-7283-5063-9 (e)

CONTENTS

BASQUE COAT OF ARMS

An Other Day An Other Time

To discover that the cycles of our lives have connected into a grander picture of cause and effect is clearly demonstrated by weather conditions and periodical tables of elements when combined make life a spectrum of visuals and physical happenings we discover by our thinking, our acting and our being who and what we think, say and do.

Upward toward a solar power downward to a seedling planted that responds to both sunlight, wind, rain, and gaseous activity that surround our every living state of cycles from birth onward to passing this living experience.

Told as children to believe in a personal faithful sense of self-expression, to live to see competitive activity be acknowledged by awards for overcoming threatening challenges of tasks that ask to provide easier access to doing our daily tasks with the least amount of debilitation.

Mentally becoming so enlightened that a process becomes a functional tool that when twisted or turned makes a bolt hold affixed to a piece of wood to build structures that make housing more protective and useful to one's daily life's motions.

Here and now, then and there, round and round moving from one place to another day another time has been life in its cultural and civilizing expansive territories that have covered one world's land masses and have brought millions upon millions of people together in a form of thought, word and deed by wireless communications. But feeling emotions must be demonstrated in words that clearly mean what we all believe in, thinking each is feeling similar to the other's meaning, purpose, and expression. We will have a greater sense of the questions asked that have come to be asked despite no one offering answers because they really don't know for sure. We take it for granted, but we believe we can fulfill what is necessary to gain a confidence by the outcomes always being the same result.

Change is putting a different button on a shirt that has a sparkly effect and calling it a fancy piece of clothing makes us look at it astonishingly and think, gee wish I had that.

Cover the cake with frosting and put nuts and good sparkles of coating on top, makes it more tasty, so that eating this delight is sure to make the feeling of being satisfied a good experience to be repeated over and over again capturing the exact moment of joy.

In the beginning was the word and the word was with god and the word was god and from then it has been word for word. Afterword before forward backward but word from the beginning came first and then afterword.....

Loving kindness always goes along way. Peace, love and joy always goes along our way with words. We exchange our thoughts, actions and deeds in words as well as being expressive about how we feel. How good it is to have the words to type to say how we feel. "Kill them all. God will recognize His own." Pope innocent III replied.

It was a crusade in the truest sense of the word, in that it had been called by the Pope. The year was 1209 and an army of thirty-thousand knights and infantrymen swept down out of the mountainous foothills of the Pyrenees in what is now South of France. The war or Albigensian Crusade lasted nearly forty years. In this war, the whole of the area was ravaged, crops burned, towns and cities razed. The intentional premeditated extermination of the inhabitants rose to such a level that it may well have constituted the first ever recorded case of genocide in European history. In the town of Beziers alone, at least fifteen-thousand men, women and children were victims of wholesale slaughter. Many were killed in the very sanctuary of the church. The infamous reply of Pope innocent III was given to one of his representatives at the scene asking how he could distinguish the heretics from the true believers.

Later, the same representative wrote back to the Pope and announced proudly that, "Neither age, nor sex, nor status was spared."

And so it came to pass in our time that another holy war would commence. One fought on a smaller scale at a subtle, more covert level. But it was a holy war, and like all wars, it was bloody.

1999 Father Heigrich Pheiffer found the veil in the church of the Capuchin Monastery in the small village in Manopello, Italy. Then Pope Benedict XVI visited the veil in September 1,2006 fabric cloth is byssus-yellowish flax referred to as sea silk-used by ancient Egyptians and Hebrews-Paul Badde the Vatican correspondent for die welt this fabric is usually only found in the graves of Egyptian Pharohs.

Otto Van Hapsburg (Habsburg) King of Jerusalem Hosannah Filio David from the root of Jesse Hosanna, to the Son of David. Vladimir Salovion-mystical philosopher the protocols of the elders of Sion a political program "The treasure of the golden triangle by Jean Luc Chaumiel published in 1979 "The Prierure` De Sion."

"The stone that creates the ripples
On the pond is simply passing through."
(unknown)

Noah hides non-Jews Septuagent Christ was Melchizadek...... I've had this manuscript for a while now. By the time it is finally known to be the truth, the whole truth and nothing but the truth. It came in the mail in one of those brown envelopes padded with bubble wrap. According to a publisher, there could be a big promotional push in the planning stage of it now. I'm not really sure how that makes me feel. I'm the person whose title is *"An Other Day An Other time"*.

And although many names have been changed most of the names including my last is still a little "windmill" unsettling. Even though much talk often during its creation, I didn't help write a story that wasn't to be true as fiction is much more believable as non-fiction in most cases. At least not the text on these printed pages.

But I was receiving dictation about these experiences as they took place in the first place. I flipped through a script. Yes, most of the names and locations have been changed as per our agreement and those who contributed to this as my mother would, word of mouth. It started eight years ago, and I'm afraid the distance between then and now isn't as comfortable as I'd hoped. Much of it seems like a dream, but the book brings back a lot of-things. Doubtless, I've grown as a person. That much is certain, but I also think that there is a great fear of being hit with the tyranny of what should occur next on a global scale.

I'm sure as with any written history some things will be clouded and discrepancies will be common. After a while, though, it really won't matter what is true and what isn't.

This tale of the second coming of Christ may, perhaps become apocryphal in magnitude to some and to others gospel and to others quite mythologically contrived in its present reality prophesied as Yeshua Messiah's returning soon.

I plan on taking the book to the park and doing my reading there. I threw it into the passenger seat of the jeep Cherokee and turn on the car radio. Rock music blares louder, and I quickly turn it to my classical station. I lend my vehicle out occasional and they forget to change it back, or so they tell me, I laugh aloud.

I have a theory that they are trying to acclimate me back to rock and roll. The meeting isn't scheduled for another few hours. I should be able to get a sufficient amount of reading in. I've already filled my daily writer's quota and am looking forward to the quiet part of the day to leisurely unfold. Thinking about the meeting causes my stomach to shift slightly, like the onset of motion sickness. I pause and gaze outside the jeep's window. For a moment, I think I see a band of air flowing in a northerly direction. Rain. The flow has a soothing effect on my stomach and then something clicks mentally. I exit the car and go back to the house. Test the handle. It's unlocked despite the small note (locked the door) taped to the other side. I notice I also left a few windows partially open. A yawn hits me and I think maybe I should have slept a little more. Either years after becoming a night person, I still haven't learned to take my napes. I put on cheap shades and become a romantic vampire about to challenge the sun. The sun in turn began to hide-and-seek among the dark sprawling clouds that appear from out of the north sky ward.

I decide to change shirts. I grab another made of virgin wool remembering when I went shopping with the rest of the family on a winter's day. It took me hours to pick out a few new shirts that day. Mom was so cool at handling my choicy moments she would hold up one for size and raise a questioning eyebrow. I would slowly shake my head and she would respond, "Don't like the smell of this one?" "Hugh".....

My typical response, "No, it doesn't taste right."

You're worse than a coach trainer after practice she said, giving me a pect of a kiss on my cheek. How vintage mom was from things that reminded me of South of France Langeduc in the Aude is where vintage wines flowed so pure and freely quenching thirsts at meal time there.

Eight years ago, I gained what has been medically documented as a elaboration or anomaly of the limbic system in the brain, termed "Synethiesia" or "Multiple Sensing." Mom merely referred to it using her special term "picky."

I got back to the closet off of the living room. All the raincoats are present. I grab them all, it will rain. I'm sure of it. I attempt to set the house alarm (another compromise) and it beeps at me irritably. It take three tries to arm it correctly. I seem to be the only one it gives problems to. An idea hits me, and I rush to my notepad. I've got one in each room for spur of the moments and or convenience sake thoughts on the run. As I'm jotting down the idea, the alarm goes off and I race back to the keypad. My ears are ringing now, and I feel the small swell of a headache begin. After two tries the alarm shuts down. A few moments later, our security company calls.

Yeah, Zack, it's me again, yeah, I know. It still doesn't like me. Well, she's not here or I would. The code is bullet. Thank you, and you have a good day. Yes, I'm sure I'll be talking to you again., "I chuckle and finished the idea. Solid, very solid. Of course, I'll have to run it through a number of people, but as executive producer and head writer. I think it'll swing. I put the notepad back out of reach of the kids on the shelf that is currently home to two Emmys and one Peabody. Not bothering with the alarm, I grab some children's aspirin on the way out. I do shut the windows. What with the rain coming the weather reports of thunderstorms coming, I didn't want to take any chances.

Traffic stops and the smell from the exhaust of the 280-z in front of me fills the air. Feeling a sneeze coming on, I quickly close off the vents and grab for a handful of unscented Kleenex. A younger me would have been frustrated and pounding on the wheel already, but no sneezing. I catch the sneeze and reach in the back for an overdue library book. I don't want to read "The second book of Daniel" in a traffic jam. My alternative selection is a travel book on the Caymans. I've read the book twice already, and a third time should be enough. We're diver certified, but haven't had a chance to go yet. The kids are old enough now that we can take them snorkeling. They're both as excited about it as I am. After a few minutes, I toss the book back in the pile. Thank God, there's a five dollar overdue limit. Traffic has gone from a snail's pace to an abrupt standstill.

A young couple climbs out of the Z. Both are dark-haired, early twenties dress in t-shirts, blue jeans and biker jackets that are road-wash free. Both lean against the car facing in opposite directions. I hear music and suddenly feel like dancing. The music swells and I climb out of the Cherokee. A few people honk as I step onto the hood and then the roof to dance. The girl looks at me funny and the guy rolls his eyes.

"Hey, man. There's no music."

He's right, I stop dancing and for a moment I debate whether or not to turn on the car radio. Instead, I hold out my hand to the girl. She shakes her head, her pageboy cut swiping the tip of her nose. I laugh and hold my hand out even further. She looks at her boyfriend and then giggles and joins me on the jeep Cherokee. We dance a minuet or as much of one as the limited space on the jeep's roof will allow us. Her perfume smells like lilacs and I fight the urge to gag. A few people cheer and honk their horns.

A cool breeze blows most of the exhaust away from the highway, and the smell of sweet rain blows around us. Another horn sounds. The car in front of the Z has moved several yards ahead. Most of the cars in the other lanes are moving slowing to enjoy the spectacle I have created.

"Let's go Cinderella," The guy shouts, opening the passenger door. The girl breaks of the dance and says, "Thank you." and gives me a quick kiss on the cheek. I take her hand and help her down.

The boy asks, "What time is it?" She holds up her wrist, sans watch. She notices mine, her eyes drifting to the small circular scars on my hands. One on each, I laugh and tell her, "I'm sorry, I've never gotten around to putting a battery in it, but I think it's about 4:37 p.m."

"He pounds the top of the Z and swears under his breath. 'Great, we're going to be late."

The driver behind me leans on his horn.

We're going to catch the new Bruce Willis flick, called "Sixth Sense." the girl says.

"Hey," I say, as she heads for the driver's side.

They both look at me.

"Why don't you two head for Mulberry Park, instead. Treat each other to a little rain mood movie you two sun lovebirds." She blushes slightly, bites her lower lip and climbs in. The boy shakes his head. "Nothing like a person who has other ideas besides ours to spoil a mood like this one." First ever time in a row row row your boat rainy spell.

Although the clouds have turned the day to gray, it hasn't begun to rain yet. Next to me on the park bench is one of the folded rain ponchos I scoot it to the far end. It's made of plastic. And smells off-color. I take out the manuscript. The pulpy smell reminds me of ripe fruit, ready to be picked off the...... it begins as I read.... tree of life.....

Suddenly Gospel of John.. The tale of the holy lance or spear of destiny as one often quoted account has it... "whomever claims this spear and solves its secret holds the destiny of the world in their hands for good or evil." British Metallurgist Robert Feather---the Spear of Christ-Jesus Christ Son of God.

David Fideler in his page 104-105 book king Rese`Angou-Marseille Gypsy Tarol Arles of the soul of the parish priests.

It was a holy war, and like all wars, it was bloody.

BASQUE COAT OF ARMS

FRANKISH KINGS
OF JERUSALEM

BASQUE COAT OF ARMS

AUSTIN, TX

J. W. Massoa looked in the mirror in her penthouse office atop the Bradford building. She ran her fingers through her hair. It had changed over the last few years from a distinguished silver with flecks of his once dominant kit black or wreath of pure white. At sixty-eight, it suited her well. Her almond shaped eyes were tinted with red, giving her baby blues an almost purple cast. Her mother was American, her father Japanese, and she found that more times than not it was a very comfortable fit among both worlds.

The gut would have to go. She prided herself on his discipline, but, despite doctors' orders, it never really extended to her diet. She tore open the package to an apple pie she kept stashed in the bottom of her desk. Massoa patted her gut. Next week, she thought.

Her office was fifteen hundred feet filled with antiques and works of art from around the globe, including a full suite of samurai armor. But her pride and joy was her latest acquisition from the Bibliotheca Reale, Turin. A self-portrait C 1514 of a balding, old man with a wreath of long white hair flowing into a long white beard. Melancholy eyes above a bulbous nose, which in turn sat above neutral lips that hinted at a frown at the corners. Well, almost my pride and joy, she thought.

A counterfeit now hung in TURIN.

Every female, Massoa thought, has her vices.

She retired the string to her sweatpants and opened a hidden closet door that blended in perfectly with the oak paneling. She wiped the sleep from his eyes and pulled out a fresh polo shirt. A few wrinkles from being hung too close to her other shirts lined the front and one of the sleeves. A few minutes with a small hand steamer aligned most of the wrinkles. She'd have Sheri take another batch to the cleaners. She glanced at her Rolex. Another two hours before she'd be in. With a small grunt, she folded up the sleeper mattress and replaced the leather cushions. What, she though, about five hours sleep? She looked at her calendar, an exact copy of the one Sheri kept on her person. There was something at one o'clock. Have to reschedule. Her nap took priority.

At her wet bar, she poured herself a glass of orange juice to wash down a multivitamin and her hypertension pill. Without thinking, she took another and touched the scar that ran down the center of his chest. She did her morning stretches, a leisurely fifteen minutes on the treadmill followed by more stretches and breathing exercises to clear her mind, and then Massoa settled in to watch the sunrise on her little empire.

There was a knock at his door.

"A little early for maid service," Massoa called out jokingly. She tucked in her shirt and buzzed the door open.

Yaphi, late twenties with a goatee and short thinning hair that curled at the nape of his neck, rushed into her office. She took a deep breath, smoothed out her jacked and tucked her tie back in. Her lungs wheezed.

"Are you okay?" Massoa said.

"Oui, sir." his accent was more pronounced than normal as he gasped for air. "It's--"

"Take another deep breath, son."

He nodded and sucked in a slow, hitching breath.

Massoa offered her glass of orange juice. "Is something wrong?"

Yaphi took the glass with a shaking hand and spilled some of the contents onto a twenty thousand dollar rug.

"Yaphi," Massoa said, "This is a Persian." She took a monogrammed towel from the bar. "It's Dr. Jacoby."

Massoa looked up the stain forgotten. "We need to replace him immediately."

Yaphi adjusted his tie and Massoa thought for a moment the young man was going to choke himself as he gasped.

"I've got a replacement in mind, sir." he handed Massoa sheaf of three-hold paper bound with brads. "Read this if you would, sir."

Massoa took what appeared to be a script of some kind, and then she noticed what it was. "Very good, Yaphi, Oh and make sure his family is given our condolences and compensated nicely. Jacoby was a fine man who shared our vision."

"Oui."

He did not ask how Jacoby died. Yaphi left and Massoa turned to the portrait on the wall. He bowed slightly. "Forgive me, Maestro" less these miscrable mortals open their eyes solemnly spoken as a truth concealed for centuries, now becoming so clear and focused.

BASQUE COAT OF ARMS

AUSTIN, TX - 2

Dr. Massoa stepped off the back deck behind her house and walked the thirty yards to her pond. The edges were muddy and filled with small potholes from where Daniel had picked most of the rocks. She laughed to herself as she imagined the pond being only abouuuuuuuuuuuuuut inches deep due to the years of Daniel skipping stones across it. Her husband and son had spent many sunsets out here tossing rocks across the glassy surface as brilliant rays of orange and yellow shot through the row of elms that lines the pond.

They were that until Daniel turned about sixteen, and then it was cars and girls and his books. Occasionally after the father/son Friday night movies ritual they would find themselves crushing a few empties and turning their attention to launching stones from the past. She remembered the look in Daniel's eyes as Tony consistently got ones to skip across the length of the pond and splashed into the opposite muddy bank. The patience of teacher and student. But Daniel never got it, although he tried many, many nights. Perhaps he would have, eventually, as he hit puberty and grew taller and stronger, but it was simply not that important anymore. Later he could lob them over the pond but as far as skipping, he never got the right combination of angle, spin, and strength. She noticed over the last few months that he'd been out there selecting a few stones. She only knew she'd like to be there to see the big splash.

After carefully moving the ceramic frog. Mr. Croak, she sat on one of the gaudy granite mushrooms they'd had since Daniel as little. Tony had purchased them on a whim. Later, they both agreed they looked absolutely trashy, but when Tony tried to move them out of sight into the garage little Daniel threw a fit. They'd been out here ever since.

She opened her mail. Bills. A letter from Daniel, one from Delores and one from TEMPLE KOUNT, INK.

The last name sparked something familiar, but she couldn't place it.

She opened the one from Delores Beachum. Just a short little form note. They see each other at least once a month at their sewing group, making quilts for the church bazaars. The note mentioned that the next meeting was going to be canceled in lieu of a special night at church. The president of the Religious Coalition of Life was going to be speaking to the members and everyone was encouraged to show. Possibly a potluck. At the bottom, Delores had scrawled in a loopy handwriting. Hi, maybe we'll get together and bake before, if you're not too busy.

Dr. Massoa folded the letter and put it back in its envelope. Her heart fluttered a little faster. And a bottle of wine. She opened Daniel's letter next. A Xeroxed cartoon of Calvin and Hobbes. Daniel's name pasted over Calvin and Hobbes on mom's shirt. She laughed and would add it to the growing collection taped to the freezer.

She opened the last letter glanced at the name at the bottom. Dr. Freilance. She skimmed the letter. Blah, blah, blah love to meet you. Discuss job opportunity, genetics, etc.

Nope.

She wadded it up and walked back into the house after setting Mr. Croak back on his toadstool.

AUSTIN, TX - 3

Delores flopped back onto her bed. She lay there staring up at the textured ceiling, her mind still reeling from her first phone conversation with J. W. Massoa.

I know things, Dr. Massoa.

Old things.

The next day they were going to meet face to face.

That night Dr. Massoa, woman of two faiths: Science and Christianity, did not sleep.

BASQUE COAT OF ARMS

"Hello?"

"Hi, Dr. Massoa this is Jimmy Kimmel how are you?"

"Fine, what can I do for you?"

"I was going to be in your neck of the woods, checking out a Texas Johnny Brown show on 6th street and thought we might be able to get together for a little follow up chat for the show. Nothing fancy, no more or anything like that. I'll treat for dinner."

"That's a possibility Mr. Kimmel I've got an interview this week. Can I give you a call in a few days?"

"Sure, no problem, I'll give you my cell number." he paused. "So you going back to the collegian circus?"

"No, private sector. Little place here in town."

"Well good luck, Dr. Massoa I look forward to your call."

BASQUE COAT OF ARMS

Massoa personally greeted Dr. Freilance in the lobby at the Bradford building. They shook hands briefly with a small bow thrown in for good measure. Massoa smiled from ear to ear. "I just got here myself." He hoisted a white bag. "Picked up some lunch for my assistant."

At times, Massoa reminded Megan and Cassia but Massoa's smile was a little warmer, the eyes filled with something less calculating. She walked her to the bank of glass elevators. The one on the left opened and stepped forward when Massoa tugged at her arm and motioned to another set of elevator doors. She swiped a plastic card and the doors swished open. "Private," she said.

"Nice," stepping in before him. "Do you own the building?"

"You as in the Japanese or as in myself?"

The doors swished shut and the elevator begun its short trip to the seventh floor. "Either/or."

"A group of Japanese investors including myself do own the building. My business occupies the top floor. Other various businesses occupy the remaining floors. But there is usually much interaction among the groups, each helping the other. In fact, the company picnics are all planned for the same day. It is my company's turn to host. We're planning on a big Texas cookout. Your entire family will be invited, of course."

"Sounds like, fun."

The keypad next to the doors beeped at each floor.

Her stomach growled. She wished she hadn't eaten as a nervous excitement tweaked her stomach. Massoa radiated a certain kind of charm. She came across as a man who had much power, but did not flaunt it opening. Instead, she was the kind of man who made every effort to play the cordial host with a hands-on attitude.

Normally, she would have felt completely at ease, but the nature and sheer absurdity of their last conversation kept floating in the back of her mind. But then again it was that conversation that got her here, when she'd pretty much already changed her mind. She realized that taking a job like this to get back at Marcos was ludicrous. But that was before she'd met this man. Massoa, driven by a mission, out of financial gain, but of religious. She could sense the power and the authority coiled just under her skin like the tensed muscles of a panther about to pounce.

But she knew he would support her decisions and yield to her expertise. No more arguing for more equipment, no more hot-wiring the outdated gear while the football team got a new stadium.

"Here we are." they made their way down the corridor paneled with real oak to set of double doors. A double key pad was sent in the wall to the right. The corridor was filled with antiques and not the kind you would find at the flea marked. She felt like she'd just stepped into Louis XIV's anteroom.

Behind a high desk, a petite woman with a long braid trailing down the back of her bright red dress looked up from behind a pair of ugly horn rimmed glasses and smiled with perfect teeth. "Good afternoon, Doctor," she said smiling and standing. They shook hands. Her dress plunged a little lower in the front she thought would be appropriate business attire especially for a Japanese businesswoman. Half Japanese, she mentally corrected herself and noticed she was also barefoot and saw a runner near her damn thin ankles that had been arrested with a shiny spot of clear fingernail polish.

"Doctors," Massoa said. "I stand corrected." She turned to Sheri as she held out her hand. "Doctor, I'm Sheri, Massoa's official hostess."

"I'm sorry," Massoa said. "Anyone who types 117 wpm is not a hostess."

She laughed softly, color flushing her freckled chest read something between them. At least with Massoa. His eyes lingered a little long and not on her perky chest, cleared her throat and despite Sheri's aerobicized body, decided she liked her.

"Yaphi said she will meet with you a little later." She handed him a manila folder. "That's it for right now, chief."

"Thank you."

"Doctor Massoa, will you be joining us for lunch today? It's rib day."

"No thank you," Dr. Massoa said. "We just got back from lunch."

"Oh," Massoa said and handed her hostess a white take-out sack.

She blushed slightly and rolled her eyes in mock embarrassment. Sheri insisted, "There better be extra sauce; There is, trust me." Massoa swiped her card and entered her office.

"She seems rather nice," Sheri said slightly baiting her. "Not what you expect from a hard-core business executive assistant."

"She's perfect," she said, in a soft voice. She went to her wet bar. "Her husband left her a year ago. She's raising twin boys by herself. I do believe they just turned three. Drink?"

"Uh, tap over ice with be fine."

She fixed two while she took in the antiques, especially the samurai armor. Her features shifted as she handed her the glass, hardened a little, became serious business for just a brief second and then he smiled and her eyes softened. She gestured to two leather couches.

"Are these all yours?" Dr. Massoa asked, nodding toward the furniture and the empty suit of armor.

"Family heirlooms, some, others I've acquired here and there. Some of my investors and colleges are very particular about maintaining an impressive image."

She studied the portrait of Leonardo Da Vinci. "That's not the real thing, is it?"

"Please, have a seat."

They sat and each took a sip. Massoa cleared her throat. "I am a woman driven by a vision. A literal vision. Perhaps I will share it with you later, should you choose to join us. I would like, however, to get you up to speed on what we are dealing with." She reached into the bottom drawer of her desk. "Would you care for an apple pie?"

"No, thank you."

She nodded and set it on the corner of the desk. "The Italian city of TURIN is a sprawling industrial conurbation. The shroud of Turin, until 1963, was housed in the Turin Cathedral which is dedicated to St. John the Baptist. It was locked there behind two iron grills above the alter of the royal chapel, nested inside three locked containers: a wooden case, an asbestos-covered iron chest, and a silver decorated wooden casket. Inside the casket, the shroud was rolled around a velvet covered staff and red silk. A backing of Holland windmill cloth was added after a fire in 1532. It's as it has been there since 1694 when the black marble royal chapel was built for the ruling Savoy family who have owned if for most of its known history. They acquired it about mid15ᵗʰ century, until 1983 when the exiled King Umbert II died. Bequeathing it to the Vatican."

"The Shroud is rarely seen. It is on the average shown only once a generation. This century it has been shown three times. Last century it was shown five times. In 1978 to commemorate the 400 anniversary of its arrival, it was put on display in a bulletproof case for forty-two days. During that time three million people filed past it."

"Didn't carbon dating in 1988 prove that The Shroud was a fake?"

Massoa smiled like a fox behind her glass of iced water. "Yes, it was, but we are getting ahead of ourselves. There were a handful of groups founded, such as the Shroud of Turin Research Project (STURP) in the USA, the Centre Internazional Di Sindonologia in Turni Cielt in France, and the British society for the Turin Shroud in the UK. Over the years, there have been dozens of books and articles published about the shroud.

"Wasn't the church against testing?"

"Reluctantly so. But eventually, The Shroud was subjected to many tests from many disciplines: historians, textile specialists, physicists, chemist, photographers, artist, art historians, anatomists, surgeons and forensic scientist—botanists. Tests included e-rays photographs, infrared light and ultraviolet spectroscopy, x-ray fluorescence. Tests yielded nothing."

"But we must bear in mind that serious scientific interest is less than a century old."

"Why is that?"

"Before, The Shroud was merely viewed as a curiosity, because the image of the Shroudman is almost too faint to make out clearly with the naked eye." All that changed in 1898 when a lawyer from Turin was asked to take the first photographs of the shroud. Secordo Pia took ten photos. It was then in photographic negative that the image suddenly exploded into focus. Instead of the vague outline, we now can see what is essentially a horrific graphic catalogue of the art of crucifixion. We now have a whole body of a bearded man with shoulder-length hair bloodied from several wounds. Small pierced wounds on the head and a round one on the only visible wrist, which is important because a body that is crucified will not support its weight with a nail through the hand. It must be nailed through the wrist. This will cause the thumb to contract toward the palm. It sold. Blood runs across the small of the back as it from a large stab wound on the chest. Several smaller flows on the front of both feet and much more on the sole of one foot.

"There are over one hundred scourge marks that curl from the back to the front of the body and legs." She took a sip of water. "It was enough to turn pia into a religious female. No artist could have created the negative effect. No known medieval artist possessed either the skill or anatomical knowledge needed to create the image."

Sheri scooted to the edge of her chair. "The carbon dating?"

She grinned. "It is exciting isn't it? Infectious." She loosened his tie. "In 1978, STURP was allowed full access to the shroud for five days. They were even allowed to take samples from the cloth. Not their objective was to discover what the image was made of and whether or not it was of human manufacture. Five million and over one hundred thousand hours of data analysis. They failed. Of course, conditions could have been better. In essence, they took the lab to the shroud as opposed to taking the Shroud to the lab and because of time constraints, many tests could not be repeated. Only one of the test s proposed by STURP was rejected by the church. Radiocarbon dating. The church's reason was the fact they feared a large portion of the cloth would be destroyed by the test. When it was pointed out that the samples already taken from the shroud would do, the church demanded that they be returned. They were locked up in the Turin Cathedral and a legal document in 1979 prevented any carbon dating.

"But after intense lobbying from several interest groups, the Vatican ran out of excuses and gave permission for the carbon dating." The Church scheduled the taking of the samples for 23 April 1988, but then the event was switched to 4a.m. 21 of April, when the Italian president was in Turin diverting press interest. Reps from the three laboratories present included Michale Tite of the British Museum

Research Laboratory. A 7cm strip was cut and then in turn three samples were cut from that. They were then sealed with control samples in a special container and then handed over to the separate labs. The whole process was videotaped."

"And?"

"The carbon dating showed that it was 99.9 per cent certain that it originated from the period 1000 to 1500, and 95 per cent certain that the cloth dated from between 1260 and 1390." he laughed and took the apple pie from the desk. Tore open the wrapper gleeful. With the snap of his jaw, he devoured half.

"I'm a little confused," Dr. Massoa said. "The shroud is a fake. Yet we're supposed to pull blood samples from it. What's the catch?"

"There are many conspiracy theories surrounding the shroud. Certain agendas are older than you would probably believe."

"There was a switch of some kind. You—"

"Are quite full of secrets. Secrets which span the globe as well as centuries. Perhaps some will be made known to you, soon."

"You're serious, aren't you?"

"Dr. Massoa I need a commitment from you. A commitment to me and this project. You will be compensated nicely for less than a year's worth of work. Of course, I know money is not a motivator to a scientist and Christian such as yourself. It is the experience, the opportunity of a (lifetime?)"

"Very tempting."

"Dr. Massoa, I'm quite sure you've already made up your mind. Otherwise, you wouldn't be here. I won't ask what happened since our last conversation, but I am going to ask you now for a commitment."

She smiled, "I think I'll take a bit of that apple pie."

Dr. Massoa	Lab Director
TEMPLE KOUNT, INK.	Project resurrection
Personal journal	Entry 13

Stage one will begin this week. I am torn between my excitement and my desire to stay objective. Massoa is either a genius with a real big secret or she is simply insane. I am fairly certain it is the former. I'm here, aren't I? Massoa has produced a burial shroud, a real shroud, or the remains of it. It is a piece of cloth nearly two feet square the edges burned from flame, accident or otherwise I have no idea. This is not the shroud she described to me or the ones I have seen in books.

There is no image on this one, just brown faded stains. She has not told me yet how it has come into her possession but with her global contacts, I can't even begin to guess.

A section of the real shroud looked like it has been rolled up and then creased. It is only a small area on the corner. This area is going to be our best shot at pulling off an available sample. Since its been folded for god knows how long there is less of a chance for "cross" contamination. But to be safe, I'll pull from several sites and run a sequencing gel.

Lysing will begin soon. I myself will put the sample under the electron microscope. I should let one of the other techs do it, and I probably will, but I'm not fooling myself into thinking I won't be there elbowing in to look at it myself. Massoa was true to his word. We have state of the art equipment. Some variations I've never seen. Prototypes from some of his colleagues. I'm sure.

Washing of the same with the EDTA solution will be next. I'll supervise. Massoa has suggested washing it twice, just as a precaution. This is the most critical stage of the operation. A mistake here will contaminate and ruin every subsequent stage. I am giddy with excitement and fear.

God help us.

AUSTIN, TX - 6

The smell of duck filled the kitchen. Daniel walked around taking in deep breaths and letting them out like a junkie huffing aerosol. "Damn, that smells good." He made a show of scooping the aroma under his nose and diving in.

Meg and Cassia stood side by side over two cutting boards slicing tomatoes and cucumbers for the salad. They both had their hair pulled back and were dressed in t-shirts and cutoffs, although Meg's were cut considerably higher showing off her runner's legs. At first glance, they could have been mistaken for sorority sisters.

"You seem to be in a better mood" Cassia said.

Daniel squeezed himself in-between them and gave each a squeeze on the shoulder. "Why shouldn't I be?" I'm dining with my two favorite girls tonight."

They both sighed in unison and then giggled.

Daniel backed off. He didn't feel jealous so much as outnumbered. "So, is Mr. I-put-on-make-up-and-got-dressed up coming for dinner?"

"Which one?" Cassia said.

"Oh. My mom the tramp." Daniel said.

Meg threw a cherry tomato at him. It struck him in the forehead and landed on the floor with a small thump.

"I'm kidding," Cassia said. "I haven't invited anyone over but you two. One man is a jerk and the other—not my type."

"That's probably all well and good." Daniel said as he opened the oven. The duck was almost ready. "Introducing possible suitors to your child is a potentially dangerous situation. If done too soon it could sway the balance of the relationship to an uncomfortable level. Scare them off. Of course, it's not like they have to change diapers or give talks on the facts of life."

"Potentially," Cassia said. She looked at Meg and they both giggled.

Daniel eyed them both suspiciously.

Meg cut open the package of cheddar cheese and Cassia began grating.

"Do you ever think about having another kid?" Megan asked. "You know, if you remarry and he doesn't have kids or you want to start another family."

Cassia laughed. "One was enough." They both giggled again. "I think I'll get any maternal urges satisfied when my son gives me a grandchild."

Meg quit giggling and Daniel stopped waving the air. They looked at each other. They stared at each other waiting for someone to say something.

"We'll probably wait a few years," Daniel said, not taking his eyes off Meg.

She winked and then they both smiled. "You know, we'll enjoy the honeymoon years and then maybe start a family."

"Yeah. Right," Cassia said.

"Now what the hell is that supposed to mean?"

"Listen to the voice of experience," Cassia said. "A couple get married. Within a year, the wife wants a baby and the husband wants a new car. Trust me."

"That's just wishful thinking on your part. All your friends have been grandparents for a few years now," Daniel said. "I think Delores is a great grandma."

They all laughed. Cassia opened the fridge. "Oops. We're out of dressing.."

"If the duck's not too close to being ready I'll go get some." Meg said.

"By the way Meg I've got your birthday present in the car. You have to open it tonight. Daniel still hasn't opened his."

"It's not my, oh, okay, I really wish you wouldn't do that, but I have to say it's very sweet and unique of you," Meg said. "I have yours stashed in the closet. I've been too busy to wrap it."

"We've got another twenty minutes," Daniel said.

"Great, I'll stop off and grab a couple of movies," Meg said. "The normal stuff, honeypot?"

"Nah", Daniel said. "Get whatever you want but nothing too sappy. No fried green magnolias, please."

"Isn't he the dreamist?" She sighed and gave him a kiss on the cheek as Daniel handed her the keys to the bullitmobile.

"Careful, the transmission's fixing to go."

Megan left and Daniel handed Cassia a bottle of wine.

"Sweetie," Cassia said. "I've got a hypothetical question for you."

"Shoot," Daniel said.

"You ever get in those situations where you don't know quite how to handle it."

"Mom, you're being a little vague."

She twisted the corkscrew into the bottle and yanked. It made a satisfying pop. "There's a dilemma at work."

"Serious, huh? Okay, let's have a seat." They took chairs at opposite ends of the table.

"You realize the ethical debates surround some of the work I've been involved with?"

"Like on the Jimmy Kimmel show?"

"Right. Now you know I firmly believe in my work. AI advances at the fertilization clinic and the GWU are going to benefit mankind. I don't have a doubt in my mind about that."

"I'm right with you. If Meg and I have a problem conceiving a grandchild for you, it's nice to know that there are alternatives, not that I have anything against adopting, and sometimes I think it would be better if the kid didn't inherit my genes, but I digress."

"The work I'm doing not at George Washington University (GWU) may be questionable."

Daniel took a sip of wine and leaned closer. "Are we talking selling baby parts, embryos for research?"

"No, nothing like that."

"Are people being used against their will—mom, you're not putting zebra heads on giraffes are you?"

She giggled and rolled her eyes.

"Are we talking mad scientist stuff?"

She scratched her chin and retied her ponytail, the silver streaks in her hair prominent. She looked around as though the duck in the oven might be taking notes despite the fact that in a few hours they would be eating it. "I know I'm being vague and pretty silly, but, well to be honest, it's kind of treading on my religious beliefs. Well, not treading exactly but I'm not going to be able to keep, well, my two faiths at a distance." she paused and laughed nervously.

Daniel shifted uneasily in his seat. "All I can really say is to follow your gut instincts. That's what you've always taught me to do." He looked at his watch, "duck's about ready. You hungry?"

Megan watched as Daniel got up and went to the oven. He was obviously preoccupied with something.

"By the way, have you found out any more about those guinea pig for money experiments?"

"Yeah," Megan said. "I got a business card in my purse."

"Thanks. A friend of mine is going to be looking into signing up for one of those college experiments for money. And I'd like to keep her informed. I mean, I don't think they'll have her chained down with her eyelids wired open and a Mary Kay make-up drip going, but–"

"Are you and her–"

"Uh, proximity friends. She hangs out at the park across from work and draws and sketches. She's kind of freaky looking. Blue hair, nose ring."

"You love those creative types."

"I kind of prefer the green thumbs to the blue hairs nowadays, don't ya know?"

"Any way, I figured you'd never get around to it, so I picked up those earrings for Meg," Daniel said. "What are you getting her?"

"Not a clue."

The tenth rock skimmed the surface of the pond,

Leaving behind a trail of six sets of ripples. With a final splash, it sank a good ten feet away from dry land. "WOW!" Daniel said.

It was after dinner and the movie. His mom had retired for the evening and darkness had fallen. Now he and Meg stood out in the back, a huge spot lighting the land like a movie set. Me sipped another glass of wine at the edge of the deck. "That was good, honey, you almost got it."

Daniel picked up another rock, turned it over in his hand and then slammed it down on the ground where it shattered against another. The chips flew and stung his leg. "Damn."

"Hey, what's wrong?"

"There's no more good rocks left," he said, exasperated. "They're all gone."

Meg set her wine glass down and walked over to him. "What's really wrong?" She could always tell, he thought. Even when he wasn't being obvious, but it was getting to be increasingly harder as the day approached. Her departure date was etched on his mental and emotional calendar. A pivotal point to be sure, hoping it would turn one way but knowing from experience that it was just as likely to fall another.

"Nothing," he said with a weak smile.

"You are a terrible actor." Her hand slid over his and their fingers laced together. "You better share. I don't want our last little week to be this doom and gloom silence. You're sucking all the sunshine out of the state."

Daniel leaned his head against her shoulder. He caught her familiar lilac scent, and inhaled slowly and deeply. "Everything's okay." he whispered and squeezed her hand.

"I hate it when you get all macho," she said softly running her fingers through his hair. "it's only going to be for a few weeks."

"I know, angel."

"Would you rather I stay?"

"Of course."

"All you have to do is ask."

"You know I wouldn't do that. This is too good an opportunity to pass up and if you stay because of me, there's a chance that nasty resentment thing will happen and I'm not going to take responsibility for that."

"I'll take responsibility for it."

"No, I want you to go and get excited about your flowers and your stems and your Latin classification and then I want you to come back and share the enthusiasm with me. I promise I'll be a good student."

She laughed. "I was rather hoping you would be bad 'cuz then I'd have to inflict some corporal punishment."

"You going to spank my behind?"

"That," Meg said. "Or I'm going to doodle on it."

"Oops. You noticed?"

"You tried being too sneaky last night, but I was awake the entire time you were using my left butt cheek as a drawing board. You used that fancy pen, didn't ya?"

"I just thought that a little flower would look really sexy there." Daniel said.

"It does. I've been careful not to wash it. Silly, huh?"

"Yip." he leaned his head up and playfully bit her on the shoulder.

She yelped and then giggled. "I love you."

"I love you too."

Meg caressed his cheek and felt something wet. She touched her hand to her mouth. Tasted salt. And then everything blurred and twin diamonds raced down her own cheek.

BASQUE COAT OF ARMS

MEMPHIS, TN

The stretch limo parted the throng of protesters outside the woman's clinic like a black wedge. Sitting comfortably in the back, head of the Religious Coalition for Life, stubbed out her cigar and crunched a breath mind. Massoa was a young, boyish looking female of thirty-nine and currently head of one of the largest religious/political movements in American. Her assistant, Sheri, went over some notes with her.

"We've got the protest now; we'll make a stop and let you do your thing," Sheri said. She cleaned her tortoiseshell glasses. "We've already gone over the speech, and I trust you've practiced it."

Massoa nodded.

"You'll speak to the crowd, hand out, and if you get arrested we'll have you out in a few hours. The press has been alerted so we'll make the nine and ten. If you don't get arrest." she smiled. "I'm sure you'll make the news one way or another Massoa adjusted her tie and took something out of her jacket pocket. "After that you've got a few days off and then a speaking engagement in let's see..."

Massoa consulted her laptop. "Austin, Texas. Actually, it's a small town right outside of Austin at one of the churches. Its President Cottrell's hometown, so I'm sure it will make quite an impression. Of course, we'll alert the smaller newspapers and it'll probably get picked up on the wire. We want this to build up slowly. The pastor of the church wants you to do your bit and make sure you include your appearance on Jimmy's show regarding the genetics show."

"Oh, yes Doctor Massoa."

Dr. Massoa tapped her lip. "Hmm. Do we still have her number on file?"

A few quick clicks of the keys on the laptop. "Yes."

"Very good."

Silence.

"The smile is coming in nicely Sheri said.

Massoa's hand went to her face, her lip, felt the thick line where the hair would not grow. Her harelip matched her boyish good looks. She had taken some advice recently and decided to grow a beard. Hadn't decided if she was going to take that leap of faith. She'd have to wait and see if it accented rather than camouflaged the small overlap of flesh. And, of course, how her counterparts (other)women thought of it was her main concern.

A cellular phone chirped. "This is Massoa's assistant, Sheri."

She held the phone to Massoa, "for you."

"Senator Freilance," Marcos said. "Something about the campaign." Massoa waved her hand. "Tell him I'll call him back."

"She's very busy right now, Senator. Why don't you call Amy back and have her set up something from next week. Yes, sir. I'm sorry. Sir probably by phone. You have a good day. Senator." She clicked the phone off. "Jerk."

"Is everything set?"

"Yes, we've spoken with Dr. Massoa. She knows we're coming."

Massoa said, "Quite the player, smart man. He'll get out a sound byte or two. What about security?"

"Taken care of. We've got Rog and her crew in front of us, just in case. Oh, the PR boys said to loosen the tie. Undo a couple of buttons."

"Why don't I lose it altogether, roll up the sleeves? Real working woman look."

"Roll up the sleeves, but just loosen the tie."

The cellular buzzed again. "No, Amy." Sheri said.

"Take a message."

She clicked off. "That woman called again."

"Which one?" Massoa chuckled, taking off her tie and rolling up her sleeves.

"Jasmine Starr."

"Damn." Massoa shook her head.

"She's not going to be a problem, is she?"

"No, I'll handle it."

They circled the crowd one more time. Various pasteboard signs proclaimed "life!" sand graphic pictures of aborted fetuses jutted out of the crowd here and there. A roar from the crowd followed them as they circled.

"I've taken the liberty of passing a few of these around the crowd," his assistant said. "Just a few here and there." he tossed a small round metal pit. Sheri turned over the button. Its face was three stripes of red, white and blue with the gold letters: "For Pres." Massoa laughed nonchalantly. "I don't know where you guys come up with this stuff."

"The Press is here," Massoa said, with a fox's smile.

"Good." Amy tossed his assistant his tie. "let's do it."

She didn't know where her assistant had dug up the soapbox, but it was effective and made a point, indicative of their grassroots strategies. Sheri plopped the box on the sidewalk leading up to the front door of the clinic and pulled out a wireless microphone. She then launched into a history of the RCL. How they took a failed the Republican Presidential Nomination Campaign mailing list and built the RCL from the bottom up, with solid foundations at the grassroots levels. She told them how they, the people with the signs, were the people with the power and how united, they changed the government at the state level and stopped the killing unborn children. She exhorted upon them the virtues of the RCL's deeds and commitments and recognized also a commitment to those children after their birth, and that the RCL meant not only life but a good life, a good solid family life and that the members of RCL recognized this, building churches and homes and letting their congressional representatives know their wishes and the consequences of ignoring those wishes. She told them of their power in Washington, of their full time lobbyists with the same morale and high ideals as themselves. "The new president will have to come to us, ladies and gentlemen!"

The crowd cheered.

"Massoa for Pres!" someone shouted.

Massoa laughed, blushing slightly, "Now, now, we all know that would be a demotion."

The crowd laughed.

"But today we are here because this is where the battle for life begins. Let us never forget that."

The crowd began their changes and started their human chains; Massoa glanced at her watch once or twice and mingled with the crowd, stopping to shake hands, only occasionally refusing to sign Sheri for Pres button. She directed a few requests for dinner and lunch to her assistant, who hung back a few steps.

Suddenly there was a commotion as a short Hispanic man with a thick dark gray suit elbowed through the crowd and made his way towards the door of the woman's clinic. "Dr. Massoa," her assistant said.

She stopped in front of a cameraman to say something to a female reporter with a slight overbite.

A few protesters broke rank and made their way to the dark-skinned doctor. One pulled a gun. Someone screamed. The cameraman kept rolling. The rest of the protesters scattered. The police drew their weapons and a small panic among the crowd spread as everyone scrambled for cover.

Massoa jogged in the direction of the reporter. Her hands up, palms open. "Sir," she said her voice deep and full of authority.

Massoa's eyes blinked wide. She held her hands in front of him, palms out.

The man with the gun spoke, "stay right there, I don't want you to get hurt!"

"Of course, you don't." She slowed her pace to a very slow casual walk. "You're here because you love life. You want to save lives."

"I'll save more if I kill this bastard," the gunman said.

"What's your name?"

Boe Constrictor.

"Where are you from, Boe?"

"San Antonio."

"Lovely place, you're a long way from home."

"I, uh, took the bus."

"Very resourceful. Boe, I'm Dr. Freilance, founder of the RCL, The Religious Coalition for Life. All life is precious. All life has potential for good."

Boe looked around.

The police moved slowly inside the chain link fence.

He licked his lips.

Massoa stepped between the gun and Boe.

"If you kill her, your life will be over, canceling out the good you too can do. You'll give the enemy something that will be used against us. They'll say the RCL kills doctors who don't agree with our philosophy. Nobody wants that. It's not too late. It's never too late."

"I'm just trying to make a difference." Boe looked at Massoa, "you can, but not like this. Give me the gun and I won't press charges." They looked each other eye to eye, face to face.

"Choose life, Boe."

The revolver swiveled on Boe's finger so that the butt of the gun faced Massoa who took it instantly. The police tackled Boe to the ground also knocking down the gun.

Dr. Massoa helped Marcos to his feet and put his hand on Cassia's shoulder. "I owe you one." commander and chief..........

Dr. Freilance, founder of the RCL, the Religious Coalition for Life. Thank you for joining us.

Audience applause. Standing ovation from everyone in the audience

Dr. Massoa, "Thank you, Jimmy."

Jimmy: "Your views?"

Dr. Massoa read the last page of the Jimmy transcript with Megan and Cassia. Perfect.

Dr. Massoa put the transcript down, rubbed the bridge of her nose and pulled out another apple pie. She buzzed Sheri.

BASQUE COAT OF ARMS

BLOOD CLOTH OF TURIN

BASQUE COAT OF ARMS

BASQUE COAT OF ARMS

San Antonio, TX

It was a slightly breezy day and the sun warmed Josie Duchamp through her thigh-length black dress as she walked across Mulberry Park to a vacant bench. She tousled her blue-black hair and tucked it behind her ears.

A few college boys playing Frisbee stared at her. One smiled. She set down her portfolio, snapped open her leather bound journal and withdrew the pen nestled in the holding strap. She touched the tip of the pen to her tongue, a habit she's known to have had since sixth grade, and put pen to paper.

On her downward spiral tablet, she wrote, as she skipped a line and continued.

> "The depth of a soul
> Is slow and inevitable.
> Like the corrosion
> Of a discarded (crucifix).
> Made out of copper
> Non-magnetic metal."

A loud gong sounded. She looked across the way and saw the church bell swaying. Touching the small gold cross hanging on a chain from her neck, she scratched out "heavy metal" and added "crucifix."

And then changed the title to "discarded crucifix."

She liked that.

As an afterthought, she did a quick doodle of Mickey Mouse hanging from a cross.

The breeze picked up slightly, and Josie put one of her shoes on the open portfolio on the park bench to prevent the plastic covered sheets from flipping. She slid out a sketch pad and popped the lid off a marker. She touched it to her tongue and instantly realized her mistake. She laughed and marked off a few squares for a story board.

The park spread out before her in a big square lot of trees, shrubs and open area. A small group of kids played kickball near the playground to her right. A few teachers and parents read books with one eye which watching the tiny Tarzans and Janes swing from the monkey bars with their roaming other eyes. Directly across from her on another park bench sat a man in his early twenties dressed in a shirt and loose tie. He munched slowly on a sandwich, a bag tucked under his thigh to prevent it from blowing away. No his other side was a package with flowered wrapping paper and a small box. With his free hand he duffled with what appeared to be a small flat rock. She wondered if he saw her faupax with the marker. Then decided it didn't matter.

She took a deep breath, felt the cool air fill her lungs, held it for a moment and let it out slowly. Here goes, kid. The first episode of *Jiggles & Stretch*. She paused and reread her letter from Nickelodeon asking to look at more story synopses. Her energy recharged, she dove in.

Ten minutes later, an orange ball rolled on the grass like a whisper and bumped her feet. She looked up.

In hot pursuit of the kickball was a pigtailed girl with big blue eyes and a smile filled with very white and tiny teeth. "Sorry about that," the girl said. She clapped her hands together wanting Josie to throw the ball. She giggled and Josie smiled despite the interruption. With a light tap of her foot she sent the ball back to its kindergarten owner. "You're awfully cute."

"I know," the girl said, cradling the ball. "I'm a princess."

"Of course, you are." Josie leaned forward. "Do you mind if I draw a picture of you real quick?"

"Can I hold the ball?"

"Sure."

The girl rocked back and forth. "What's in your nose?"

"A nose ring."

"It looks silly."

With a few quick strokes, Josie drew a fine new caricature of her new friend. She showed it to her.

"That's me," the girl said. "I look silly."

"We're all silly," Josie said. "Here, you can have it."

"For six dollars?"

"Six dollars?"

"That's how much they cost at Six Flags Fiesta Texas. Six dollars."

"No honey, this one's free."

"Thanks," she said and scampered away.

The little girl blended back in with the crowd of kids, showing off her new picture. Laughter filled the air, and Josie envied it. She'd like to have a little girl and a little boy. Cliché', but one of each please. Yeah. Right, she thought.

A shadow fell across her sketchpad near the end of her second storyboard. Before she looked up, her nose caught the scent of men's cologne.

"Hi. Cool hair! Do you play in a band or something?" It was one of the frat boys. Idly tapping the Frisbee against his thigh like a silent tambourine.

"Purple," Josie mused aloud. "No, green. Definitely a green Fruit loop."

"Fruit loop? I don't get—"

"Look, Farmer Ted. I'm not interested in men, let alone some idiot frat boy, so quit holding your stomach in. You look ridiculous."

"A lesbo. That's cool." He seemed confident that the problem was not him.

"Run along little boy."

He muttered something under his breath and trotted off.

She quickly added the finishing touches to the last panel of the story board. Something was missing, some element in the story she couldn't quite put her finger on. Evidently, Nick liked what they saw, but something still nagged at her. Josie pulled the prized letter out again, reading it with mystical awe. Savoring it each time as if with each read word it began to fade like a forgotten dream.

Something caught her attention. Something clicked out not obviously. She saw the dealing in her mind's memory. She didn't remember it being the 18th, she though it was the 19ᵗʰ. She pulled out her check book and looked at the little calendar. She thought she was all right and then she looked at the year. She was looking at last year's calendar. A hot ball of lead dropped in her stomach. She looked around. Saw a shop a FedEx sign glowed in the window.

A black man with a stocking cap and toothy grin smiled at her as she headed for the copy shop. She couldn't tell what the man was wearing. The sign that read "open" hid the clothes underneath. A dog dozed in the shade of a tree behind him.

"Excuse me, miss,' he said.

"One step ahead of you." Josie showed her gold cross.

"Bless you, sister," he said as she passed him.

She halfway expected him to smell of rotten fruit, but instead cause a whiff of that stuff that comes in the white bottle with the little ship on it. "Asshole," she muttered out of earshot.

She stepped into FedEx and instantly felt the temperature drop several degrees. The second thing she noticed was a pulpy smell of paper. With her portfolio under her arm, she plowed her way through the line, acting as if she'd phoned ahead and made reservations. A blonde man, mid-twenties with a light beard and blue eyes approached her. He wore a rumpled shirt and a loose tie. The top button of his skirt was undone. A black plastic nametag hung upside down. Daniel.

She recognized him as the sandwich eater at the park, the one with the mystery present.

"Hi," she said.

He leaned forward on his elbow. "There's one thing we all learned in kindergarten and that was–"

He paused for half a beat.

"–to wait your turn in line. You're more than welcome to stand here at the counter, but I'm afraid that angry mob of people won't allow much more. I warn you I've seen them break out torches and pitchforks."

"I've got to get this stuff copied and overnighted today."

"I like your hair." Blue/black. Like hair in the old four-color comics. Black with blue highlights.

"Thanks and shipping?"

"There's a drop box over by the door. Fill out an air bill with all the pertinent information. As soon as you're done we'll get started on the copies."

Dr. Massoa, there are already 10,000 frozen embryos floating around in liquid nitrogen baths in the US which is one of the few countries in the world where you can see sperm and eggs. We already have catalogues at fertility clinics that list the characteristics of sperm donors, including one made up of Nobel Prize winners. Without regulation it will only be a matter of time before some entrepreneur tryst to market embryos derived from Cindy Crawford or Michael Jordan. Think about it. This will become a screening process. If you don't cut the grade you will be aborted. Your existence terminated before you have a change to overcome whatever it is that marks you as less than perfect.

(Should be noted that Marcos had a harelip and speaks with a slight lisp)

Jimmy is that the next step?

Of course, it's a very real and probable step. Your genes will be mapped out for you and this information will be sold to potential employers. What do you think your chances of getting hired at a job that will give you the opportunity to support your family are if there is a chance in your genetic code of your coming down with a debilitating disease, one that will cost the company insurance time and precious money. Information, that is the hot commodity of the future and if you don't believe it you are only kidding yourself.

Dr. Massoa: so the best way to produce a crack seal team or a group of astronauts is to clone the appropriate mix of sperm and egg and wait twenty years. I don't think so. This isn't Nazi Germany—

Dr. Massoa: hah, in Germany an experiment like the one you performed, doctor, would be considered a felony and punishable by up to five years in prison.

Audience applause

Dr. Massoa: then it's a good thing we live in America.

Audience applause, boo, boo.

Dr. Freilance: we don't need the government to do this. We've got the private market to make the nightmare scenarios a reality. And that's where our worst fears are going to become true. More than 25 countries have commissions that set policy on reproductive technology. In Britain, our ally, cloning human cells requires a license the governing body refuse to grant. Violators face up to ten years in prison. In Japan, research on human cloning is prohibited by guidelines that in the country's conformist society have the force of law.

Jimmy: "And how exactly was the funding provided for? Taxpayer dollars, Doctor?"

That's true, but in this country, Satan's work is done and those who disobey god's will are left to be free in the streets.

Jimmy: "Mr. Kimmel, please."

Dr. Massoa: George Washington University is privately funded. I'd like to add that as a fellow Christian I'm pleased with the RCL and Dr. Freilance.

It is mister, isn't it? And their efforts to act as a sounding board for the inevitable ethics issue which will arise from this. Thank you, Dr. Freilance. I'd also like to point out that many people from all walks of life and faiths will benefit from this procedure should it work.

Jimmy: this hasn't been performed in normal cells?

Dr. Massoa: not to my knowledge.

Jimmy: You're not with Boe anymore?

Dr. Massoa: "I've resigned my post there to spend more time with my son."

Loose comment! "It's a abomination of God's Will!"

Jimmy: "Let's see how our audience feels about this shall we?!"

Man in audience: "Yeah, I have a question for the woman doctor?"

Dr. Massoa: "Yes?"

Man: "Can you use your technique to put a zebra head on a giraffe?"

(At this point in time, a pizza delivery man walks on the set with two large pizza boxes. Jimmy pulls out a twenty and exchanges it for the pizza.)

Jimmy: "Anyone hungry?"

Audience applause.

Jimmy: "But seriously folks, "I have here an issue of Time Magazine where your former partner Dr. Freilance reported that his technique could produce human clones within 'a minimum of a couple of years.'"

Dr. Massoa: "Like I said, I am no longer with GWU although, I still support their work and speak occasionally with the research and development cloning team."

Jimmy: "Okay, and you said earlier that you had a son."

Dr. Massoa: "Yes, I have one son, Daniel. A very bright young man. He's attending college in San Antonio."

Jimmy: only one child?

Dr. Massoa: "Yes, and I think I know where this is headed."

Dr. Massoa: "So if you had a freezer full of Daniel embryos would you still only be the mother of one son?"

Dr. Massoa: "Oh yes, he's more than enough."

Jimmy: "And that's all the time we have for today. And now my food for thought. It is becoming increasingly apparent that in the years to come as genetic engineering and cloning begin to converge that the researchers exploring these frontiers will have to become ethicists as well as scientists. Technology tends to develop a momentum all its own. The time to discuss whether it is right or wrong is before it has been put to use. Not after. And that's my food for though. I'd like to say thanks to my quests and pizza hut for the wonderful snack. Tune in tomorrow for celebrity escorts/skin's the truth."

"You're a little short for a storm trooper," Josie said, taking her hair down.

"Star war," Daniel said. "1977, although the comic book version was published in 1976."

Her eyes widened. "Very good. You're quick."

"Actually, that's not your next line but I digress."

And Josie felt herself smile for the second time today. Could very well be a new world record.

A short, frumpy looking woman with a baby clinging to her hem touched Josie's necklace. "That's a beautiful cross. I have one almost like it."

Josie winked at Daniel and turned to the woman. "Yeah, well, I've got a newsflash for you. If your precious little savior had been executed the state today instead of a couple thousand years ago, you'd now be wearing little electric chairs around your neck–"

"Texas uses lethal injection," Daniel said matter of fact.

"Even better. Some entrepreneur would make little working syringe necklaces and everyone'd have their own little needle and the cops couldn't check them because of religious beliefs. Roman Catholics would be wearing the electric chairs with little crispy Jesus(s). And in Mexico, there'd be a church that winds up on CNN because the electric chair Jesus they have they will have smoke coming out from its eye sockets or the syringe in the church will be dripping blood. Suddenly, it's another miracle."

The woman paled and crossed herself. "you don't know what you're saying. You're young."

"I'm kind of partial to the syringe idea." Daniel said.

"More people have gotten closer to god with drugs than sitting in a local Baptist church being told they're going to burn in hell for dancing."

"Baptist?" Daniel said.

"You've got to respect the Indians and their church with the peyote thing. At least they're not kidding themselves." Josie turned to Daniel, evidently dismissing the Hispanic woman and her child. "Hi, I'm Josie. You guys hiring?"

"What are you going to miss about me?"

Daniel let a few heartbeats of silence pass as he envisioned not being able to call her and hear her voice. Not being able to hug her and plant baby kisses all over her neck and shoulders. Not being able to feel the smooth, taut skin on her back.

"I expected a more immediate response." Megan said. She sat behind a desk with textbooks laid open on her lap, her runner's leash propped on the desk. Her skin was the color of lightly creamed coffee that made her chocolate brown eyes stand out even more as she stared at Daniel through her reading glasses. She ran her fingers through her thick wavy, dark blonde hair and pulled it back into a loose ponytail.

Megan occasionally cursed the natural curl of her hair, wishing it was straight, but generally she was quite content with her mulatto heritage. Her mixed genes had provided her with skin and hair that were basically maintenance free, allowing her to concentrate on Daniel, her studies, and running. She didn't consider herself beautiful by any means, (although, she was becoming increasingly more proud of her legs), more of a plain if not mousy type. She often described her face and hair as one brush stroke of bland. Of course, she was hard on herself, but she admitted she felt beautiful when she smiled or laughed.

And Daniel made her laugh often, as people in love often do.

Meg's apartment was a two bedroom with the smaller room serving as a study/office. Daniel was currently curled up on a small couch reading through a stack of children's picture books.

Megan, until a moment ago, had her nose buried in a book entitled: wildflowers of the southwest. She wore one of Daniel's t-shirts and a pair of baggy shorts that barely stayed on her slip hips. The shorts were from a time before she took up running, when she'd lay down on the bed and pull the zipper up with pliers.

"Hello," she said.

"Your smell,"

"I smell?" Mcgan asked.

"No goober. I'm, going to miss your smell."

"Buy a bottle of perfume."

Daniel put down his book and placed a flat rock the size of a cookie on the book to mark his spot. "No, not your perfume. It's more of a combination of things. The soap you use with your clothes, your natural body smell. It's very subtle. It's one of the first things I noticed about you when I got close enough. Now it's one of the last things to fade away. Thirty minutes after you've left, I can cup my hands together and still smell you. And I don't mean that in a sticky finger kind of way. It's like the time you snuck into my apartment and hid in the closet and were going to scare me."

"And you scared me first. I thought you were kidding when you said you could smell me when you walked by."

"Nope. I smelled lilacs."

"Syringa Vulgaris." she beamed and the blandness washed away as color flooded her dimpled cheeks and her smile pushed them up into two cute little balls. Her eyes lit up, seeming to push away the harsh shadows. "That's very sweet."

"Just a personal thing. I love you."

She took her glasses off and turned out the light. Curls up next to him on the couch. "I know a veryyy personal thing and I mean it in a sticky finger kind of way, honeypot." Josie undid the top button on his pants.

The afternoon started off pleasant enough at the basketball court next to the church. The crowd of children abandoned the adjoining playground and gathered next to the court where they gleefully counted down in unison.

"Six."

Marcos passed the basketball between his legs, sweat flying from his brow and arms onto the cracked blacktop. His eyes flicked to Milisha, a twelve-year-old black girl wearing a NY giants jacket three times bigger than her. She was the official timekeeper, the blue stopwatch held in her little hands. She nodded to Marcos. Sometimes the crowd had a tendency to start counting down when it wasn't anywhere near time to start counting down.

Force a bad pass or weak shot. Change of possession with enough time on the clock to give the other team a chance to score.

"Five."

Rasheed took a step forward, loose rocks grating under his six fourteen sneakers. "Come on, Mark_o, take it to the hole. Gotta come through me."

Marcos smiled at the young African-American. They'd been dogging each other for close to forty-five minutes now. His heart was pounding at its peak rate. At forty-eight, Marcos was in remarkable shape.

"Four."

Marcos dipped his shoulder left and charged right. Rasheed went for the feet and in the an attempt to recover, caught his sneaker on the uneven asphalt.

"Three."

Putting his weight into the charge, Marcos bumped Rasheed, knocking him to the ground. Rasheed yelled foul. The crowd roared.

"Two."

Robbins, the six ten giant of the city court, smirked. "Come to papa."

Marcos went to his right and launched himself toward the basket. Robbins followed and Marcos dished the ball off behind his back in mid-air to Tony G who smiled a mouthful of crooked teeth.

"One."

He let a smooth jumper float toward the hoop. Robbins and Marcos hit the ground together. Robbins turned in time to see–

"buzzzzzzzz."

–nothing but net.

The crowd cheered. The twins. Robbins and Rasheed, slapped high-fives laughing to themselves. Tony G acknowledged them with a nod of his chin and pulled up his baggy shorts.

"Damn, Marcos that was some cold-blooded shit." Rasheed said. Massaging he chest where Marcos had planted the elbow.

"No autopsy, no foul." Marcos feigned the move again. "Besides, your big old feet weren't planted."

Robbins laughed and slapped Rasheed on the back.

Marcos grabbed a towel and wiped the seat off his arms, a tattoo of a bulldog on his right bicep. The letter semper fi inked underneath. "You don't have any room to be shooting off at the mouth. Robbins. Not with those ski boots of yours."

Robbins smile shrunk to a grin. "One of these days, I want to see you take it to the hole. All the way."

"On the wings of angels, my boy."

The church bell tolled.

Marcos looked up wiped his face

Tony G came up and patted him on the back. "Smooth as silk."

"I knew you'd be there." Marcos said. "I though Rasheed might get back up in time to reject the shot."

"Shoot. That fool spends too much time on his butt flipping channels to take me to school. Bid old potato chip butt."

"Hey, father Marcos," Rasheed yelled. "You mind if we keep the ball a little longer?"

"Nah, bring it over when you're done."

"Cool."

He put his collar back on. A new youth joined the crowd; his face scanned the others. He was about seventeen-years-old. Gansta colors.

"Friend of yours?" Marcos asked Rasheed.

He shrugged. "Probably heard about the great white priest and his divine dunking"

They all laughed.

"Just don't let him walk off with the ball," Marcos said.

There was a tiny pop. For a brief instant Marcos though it was a firecracker, but he knew the neighborhood enough to know bullets were flying. The kids screamed.

Another pop and Marcos felt himself thrown to the ground. His head thudded against the concrete. Stars flared and dimmed. He blinked is eyes.

Rasheed was on top of him. "You okay, father. You ain't hit?"

Marcos took a quick mental inventory. Heard the screams of running kids. "don't think so."

"Good, good," Rasheed said. "Nothing happen to my man on the court."

"Rasheed, I'm fine," Marcos said, "Let me up."

"I can't." tears streamed from Rasheed's eyes. "I can't feel nothing`. I can't move."

Marcos rolled Rasheed over. A pool of shit and piss and blood formed around his lower back.

"Medic!" Marcos called. The word surprised him. So easily, it formed on his lips my god. He glanced around for his bag. He grabbed his towel and tried to stifle the wound, his combat training coming back to him. He pulled his cellular out and hit 911.

"Ymf", Robbins said. "God, not Rasheed, too. Oh my brother, my brother, my brother."

"Too?", Marcos said.

Robbins motioned over to the court. He didn't recognize the body. Half the face was missing. He did recognize the giant's jacket. And the stopwatch. Robbins face screwed up with anger. A bit of snot ran down his upper lip. He wiped it with the back of his hand, the fingers wrapped around the handle of a 9mm. Beyond Milisha's body, he saw the gangsta colors of the stranger on the ground dragging his left leg as he crawled like a three-legged turtle.

"I winged the slow punk." Robbins said. He walked toward the downed kid, stepping over Melisha's body. The stopwatch crunched under his foot.

Rasheed whimpered. "Save me father." His eyes glazed over, fixed on some point in space.

"Where's the medic? Hang in there, kid!", Marcos said, as he held Rasheed's hand.

"Father....?" Rasheed blinked twice and died.

Another pop. Father Marcos turned in time to see Robbin's smoking 9mm pointed at a little red fountain jetting from the new kid's head.

Afterwards, Daniel rolled over and patted Meg on her rear end. "Get a tape recorder for this."

She murmured something and snuggled up closer to him.

"I'm trying to have a moment here." Daniel said.

"Sure, honeypot," Meg said, through a pillow. "Recording."

"I think we should live together."

She perked up slightly. "Like sharing closet space and scolding each other for leaving the lights on?"

"Or the iron."

"Hey," she said. "I've been doing really good about that lately."

"You left it on earlier today when I came over."

"That's cause I knew you'd be needing it."

"Anyway...."

"Yes, I'll move in with you." she scooted even closer to him, pushing him against the wall. Took his hand and pulled it over her life a safety belt. Added, "when I get back from the trip," and promptly fell back asleep.

Daniel scrambled the eggs, while Meg showered after her morning run. As he was adding some grated cheese, she padded into the kitchen, a towel wrapped around her body and a smaller one around her head. She picked up his rock on the counter. "Make it yet.?"

"Not yet. I'm waiting. Oh" he said changing the subject. "You missed it a few days ago," Daniel said. "At work one of the customers went off on another customer. This chick all in black like those death chicks from high school went off on this lady who touched her crucifix necklace. Lady didn't even know what hit her."

She patted her wet hair with the towel. "Was she pretty?"

"Might have been. She was kind of crusty–"

"No, the girl–"

"That's who I meant she was –et."

"Really?"

"Okay, she was decent looking if you're into blue hair. She's evidently got some deal in the works. I'm no sure what. Some cartoon thing."

Meg grabbed a fork and took a bit of the eggs. "More cheese. Did you tell her about the children's stories you're working on?"

"Nah." Daniel sprinkled more cheddar on her eggs. "She seems further along than I am and you know she's probably had a thousand nut cases barrage her with bullshit."

"Jealous?"

"Nope. Totally different area."

"Success is success."

"Don't mean nothing until you sign on the dotted line."

"You like her, don't you?"

"I told you. Paranoid woman, she was just okay looking."

"Yeah, but that physical stuff's never really been your bag. I know how much you hate those Barbie types. She's creative, and that's a turn-on for you."

"Well–"

"Lord, knows why you're interested in this botanist."

Daniel moved the eggs off the burner, set down his spatula and grabbed her in a bear hug. "I find the geeky little scientist inside you totally compelling. The way your eyes light up when you get excited talking about your cross pollination and cloning. Your face gets all flushed like when you laugh or are on the verge of an orgasm. You get that look sometimes when I just hold you. Like now. Makes me feel special."

"Um, you're good. So what's her name?"

"Didn't catch it, Daniel said, planting a row of kisses along her bare shoulder."

BASQUE COAT OF ARMS

SAN ANTONIO, TX - 2

Daniel unwrapped his ham and cheese sandwich. Bits of lettuce fell to the ground. He kicked them away with his foot, not wanting a colony of ants trekking up his leg. He took a bite of the first hand and checked his watch. Twenty more minutes of his break left. His left hand absently plucked at the bow to the wrapped present, feeling the silky texture of the spiraled curls. A few minutes later, ants covered the lettuce he'd kicked away. The trail of red dot ran off to the left over a small dandelion. Megan would know the Latin name for the yellow flower. He thought about her leaving next week for her ten week field course in southwest wildflowers. His stomach turned hot and sour.

Being in love hurts, he thought.

Her birthday was coming up. He wanted it to be special something he'd never done for anyone maybe he could write a children's book about a girls and her flowers yeah, but to him it wouldn't have any real impact unless it got published and then he could dedicate it to her. But he knew when and if he ever got published, he would dedicate it to his mother and father. After all, they'd been there for him from the start, encouraging him. They even accepted if when he told them he was going to drop out of honors calculus class in high school. They were just pleased that he decided to go to college and become what he referred to as a member of the useless degree society.

Makin' copies.

Creative minds rarely pay. But the job kept his car on the road a '67 mustang fastback painted British racing green with a vanity plate: bullet. Daniel was a big Steve McQueen fan. When he'd bought the Mustang a few years again, he'd almost gotten a Cadillac convertible. But he decided that if he bought that care, he'd have to hit the road and start a life of crime. It was definite road movie kind of car. Something about that really appealed to him it was the idea of movement that appealed to him. Everything you owned right there in the back of your car. Completely self-sufficient. Going where you wanted. California, New York, Montana, Florida. See America. Write stories on the road. Travel seldom fails to inspire a writer. That's what he'd read once, anyway.

But travel takes money. Hotels, motels, and that food thing. He sighed. It wouldn't really be that much fun without someone to share it with. Meg would have fun for about the first week. Maybe longer if they found enough flowers growing on the side of the road. And she knew she had a place to come back to. But the way he felt right now, getting away. Really appealed to his rebelliousness. He thought of his friends back home in New Mexico, jobs, mortgages, car payments. Thought about how trapped they were. But a part of his brain, the part he had to slap down every so often spoke up. Yes, but they've got money to go on vacation. That's what people do. They go on vacation. Once or twice a year. Sometimes they go out of the country.

Where the hell am I going to be in five years? He thought. Ten?

He didn't know. What he did know, was that the 'Stang was going to need a new transmission soon.

A shadow fell over him.

He looked up. It was the death chick. He moved his present and gestured for her to sit.

She did. "Hey, thanks for helping yesterday."

"No sweat," Daniel said. "You think they're going to like your stuff?"

"They liked it enough to ask to see more." She crossed her legs, ran her fingers through her hair. "It's a good sign."

"I'm a writer."

"Really," she said evenly. "Gay fiction?"

"Funny," Daniel said. "Children's books."

"Tough market," she commented and took out her journal. Popped it open, took out her pen and touched it to her tongue.

"Did that marker permanently dot your tongue?"

"This is an ink pen."

"I'm talking about the other day you had that marker."

"I don't know what you're talking about."

Daniel laughed. Closed his eyes and let the sun warm his face. "Sure."

He heard her scribble something in the journal.

"You should consider yourself lucky," Josie said.

He opened one eye.

She adjusted her nose ring. "I find most people boring."

"I'd have to meet someone you find exciting."

"Hmm."

Silence, save for pen against paper.

"FYI: we're not hiring, but I'll ask around."

"Thanks."

He heard more scribbling.

Daniel checked his watch.

"Brandon," Josie said, softly.

Daniel sat up slowly and stretched. He knocked the present off the bench.

"Pardon?" he picked it back up.

"His name was Brandon, and he was a very exciting guy. In fact on occasion, I think I bored him."

"Sounds like you were dating a Martian."

"Sometimes I thought he was from another planet. I never thought anyone would totally accept me for who I was and what I wanted to be. He accepted me so much that I actually calmed down some. I didn't need to dress so outrageously. I did the stuff I liked and enjoyed as opposed to the things I thought would get attention."

"Sounds like a hell of a guy."

Her eyes focused elsewhere. "Very great." she fidgeted with her gold cross. Kissed it slowly.

"He left you."

"Yes." she put the pen down on the bench. Tapped the closed journal to her mouth, her other hand rubbing the cross. "Left me all alone."

"That shit happens."

She barked a hoarse laugh and her eyes misted up for a moment like after a harsh sneeze. "He hit a highway embankment. Wasn't wearing his seat belt. His head was driven partially into his chest cavity. What was left of the head–I couldn't recognize him. I identified the body by this tiny tattoo he had on his ankle."

"Sorry, I had a feeling that I'd said the wrong thing."

"No, you were dead on with your assessment of the situation." She paused. "I think you would have liked him. He was a very gentle person. Very open-minded. Rapier wit, well read, but didn't mind just getting silly occasionally. Keep his inner child and his intellect very well balanced and adjusted.

"He must've been a neat person."

"He was."

Daniel checked his watch. He was going to be late. Oh well. I used to have this philosophy about my life at the beginning of college. A death short of tragedy, a marriage short of farce. I had my ups and downs like everyone else, but nothing really important. Nothing that hit either end of the spectrum. No identifying event. Something I could plant a flag on top of and say, "Yes. It was a challenge and climbed it. "This is me. This is what I'm capable of."

Josie nodded her head. "I first saw you here in the park. Pondering life. I though, there's someone waiting for something important to happen."

"My dad was killed three years ago in December. Every other Friday he and I would go to the movies. Spend some quality family time. I'd usually meet him or maybe even go grab a couple of beers with him beforehand. One Friday I canceled. I'd met this girl in my zoo class. Very cute. Great natural look a little heavier than I was usually interested in super sharp and smelled terrific. Just like lilacs. She helped me make it through the class and I asked her out after finals for Saturday night. She already had plans so I asked her out for Friday and she accepted. I canceled plans with my dad. He was cool about it even though we'd planned all month to see this movie. He was pissed, but didn't yell or anything. And he was killed that night. By a drunk driver. I didn't know until after I got back from my date with Meg."

"Jesus, what a first date!"

"She's going to be moving in a couple of months. We've skirted around the idea of marriage. Sometimes I think that maybe it's the guilt that keep us together. Just fleeting thoughts really, but occasionally it creeps in. Maybe she feels guilty because if she'd turned me down, my dad would still be alive, but, you see, if I'd gone with him it might have been both of us in that wreck. It was on the same rod on the way to our usual theater. But I wasn't there with him."

"You feel guilty for not being with him!"

"I feel guilty because the last time I talked to my father I pissed him off." He turned the package over slowly in his hands, the box rotating on opposite corners against his palms. "I think about that night. How many little variables played a part. Was I supposed to lose my dad only to gain Meg? There has to be some higher force at work. I have to believe for my sanity that there was a reason that I wasn't in the car with him. That there has to be some part in some plan for me. And I'm not talking about the part where I was spared so that I can help some old lady cross the street so she can get to the other side so she can buy a teddy bear for her granddaughter."

Josie put away her journal. "Maybe the granddaughter is autistic and for whatever stimulation reason, the bear provides her with a sense of constant security. Maybe even gives her a connection to the real world and pulls her out to the real world."

"I'm going to be a little more selfish than that. I need to see the results. And I'm sure you've had to deal with those same feelings."

She said nothing for a moment, "and you and Meg are still together?"

"Yep."

"Going to get married?"

"Hope so."

She smirked. "Kind of ironic. You getting your death and seed for your farce all in one evening."

"That's crossed my mind several times."

"If you had to pick the say things happened. If you could reverse–"

"No. I'm not even going to play what if? I value my sanity. There'll always be the game of why? I don't need to make room for what if?"

"So, she's legit cool. Eh?"

"A botanist. She'll be taking off for two and a half months with her graduate class to study southwestern wildflowers."

"She doesn't bore you?"

"Are you kidding?" he plucked the dandelion, disrupting the ant brigade and proceeded to point out the parts of the flower.

"I'm very impressed."

"And on top of that she's got great legs and a sense of humor."

"I'm very impressed."

"Thanks. You should be."

"Anyway," Josie said. "Let me ask you this are you still with—what's her name?"

"Megan," Daniel said.

"Nice," Josie said. "So what do you like best about her?"

Daniel steepled his fingers under his nose. "She makes me feel like a leading man."

"I see. That's her present?" She asked. Indicating the wrapped box.

"Actually, her birthday is coming up and Megan's got this thing where every year around her birthday she buys presents for other people. Kind of as a thank you for those she felt helped her in some way make it to her next birthday."

"Now that's original," Josie said, sincerely. "Planning on opening or just molesting the bow?"

"I'm trying to wait until she's gone. Gonna be my Meg booster."

"Cute."

"Very cute, but I still haven't figured out what to get her or what to do creative block."

She nodded, understanding that part of it. "Well, it's been nice chatting, I must run and I'm sure they're pining for you at work." She shook his hand and strolled off.

The night of Dr. Massoa's speaking engagement,

Spent a little extra time doing her hair and make-up. Daniel was visiting, having driven the hour drive up from San Antonio for dinner. Meg was having dinner with her folks and the scheduling didn't quite work out for the both of them to be together..

Daniel flipped through the cable channels, one of the many luxuries of home. He noticed the pile of workout tapes in front of the VCR. He dug his fork through another helping of lasagna. On the coffee table in front of him was a list of ideas for Meg's birthday. All were crossed out. The phone rang. Continued to ring. Daniel cocked his head down the hall. He waited for his mom to appear. When she didn't he answered the phone.

"Hello?"

"May I speak to Dr. Massoa, please?"

"The doctor's not available right now. Can I take a message.?"

"This is Jimmy."

"Cool show, sometimes."

(whispered) "Henri De Montpesat will be king of France restored circuit magazine at that time 1970 in Switzerland Lake Loman."

"Thank you. Look, I was wondering if you could give her my personal pager number. Have her page me at her soonest convenience."

"Sure thing." Daniel wrote down the info and hung up. Just then, Meg emerged from the back.

"Wow," Daniel said. "Hair looks great. Make-up too."

She smiled and did a little turnaround. She wore a dark blue flower print dress, cut slightly low in the front. Her hair was piled on top by some means Daniel couldn't figure out with two spirals of silver hanging down, framing her face.

"So what's up? I know you're not getting all dolled up for your little sewing circle meeting."

She checked her hair again in the hallway mirror. "There's a speaking engagement tonight at the church."

"And?" Daniel said.

She didn't reply.

"And," Daniel said, setting his plate aside. "You're either trying to impress someone in either the 'look at what you could have, or the look at what you can't have.' Now which is it?"

Delores smoothed out the front of her dress. "You're too damn smart for your own good."

"And?"

"And I don't know yet."

"You've lost some weight too haven't you?"

"Ten pounds," she beamed.

Dr. Massoa took IH-35 north to the first Methodist Church outside the city limits. The parking lot was filled to capacity. Her heart began beating fast and she tried to will it to slow down. She still wasn't sure what she was going to say to him. For a moment, she considered getting back in her car and going back home. She thought she might play a game of scrabble with her son.

She sat near the middle on the end to give her a clear view of him as he spoke. It was a good speech. A little on the short side and maybe a little more political that she'd expected. Delores sat next to her and several times throughout the speech prodded her in the ribs with a bony elbow. "I think he's staring at you." she whispered. And she was right. His eyes me hers.

She cocked an eyebrow. Yes, it's me.

Delores poked her again, "you two didn't... Did you?"

After the speech, there was a five minute standing ovation. Hundreds stood, gave a courtesy clap and watched the congregation light up. She saw faces full of drive and desire and purpose. But she knew that after the flash the fir would catch with some of them. She had to admire his charisma, his power. She noted the beard he was now sporting and wondered if that was due to her suggestion.

Dr. Massoa spent several minutes shaking hands and signing autographs and getting his picture snapped with several members of the sewing circle.

"He's a hunk." Delores declared. While others noticed several younger female members crowding him. As he slowly made his way towards the door, she carefully positioned herself so that their paths would intercede.

"I'd like to have me some of that," Delores said. Then looked at him staringly, "but standing next to your cleavage. I don't think he's going to notice me."

Dr. Massoa gave out handshakes and hugs right up to her cell phone. She snapped a quick photo of both he and Delores.

After a moment's hesitation, glancingly held out his hand to greet her's. A questioning filled his eyes.

"Nice smile," Delores said, taking her hand.

She tugged at it playfully. Her finger floated briefly to her harelip. "Massoa, I'm sorry," Cassia said, noticing Dr. Massoa.

"You two have met before," Delores said.

"Yes, we met on the Jimmy show Delores said. And then her trademark smile appeared.

A different kind of charm lit her eyes. She squeezed her hand.

"Oh, yes, I remember." Delores said. "Caused quite a stir around here, let me tell you."

"Can image," Massoa chuckled. She returned to Cassia."

"You're not still actively involved with any of that cloning nonsense, are you?" She started to release her grip on her hand, but she held firm.

"Oh, no. She's just living in Austin, spending some time with her son. She's widowed you know," Delores said.

Over her shoulder, and stepped light on Delores' foot, who hushed. The Jimmy leaned in. "I'm pregnant with your child and just thought I should let you know." "She said in a conspiring voice." Delores gasped. A few others followed suit. Jimmy said nothing. Instead, he pulled back through the doors to the lobby area. A few people dressed in their Sunday best followed them. He looked around, smiling and told them he'd be back in a moment. They made their way to the small kitchen that smelled of cleaners and fried chicken.

Jimmy loosened his tie. Patted his brow with a silk handkerchief from his breast pocket. "You're kidding, right?", Jimmy said.

Delores shifted her weight to one leg and crossed her arms. "and if I wasn't?"

Jimmy looked around as if the walls might be bugged. He lowered his voice. "I thought you said you had your tubes tied."

The door plopped open and the assistant poked his head through.

"Mike–"

"In a second, Blake."

Jimmy's eyes flicked to Blake's. He opened his mouth to speak, but out-back kicked the door and Massoa disappeared.

"Whether my tubes are tied or not isn't the point."

"It's exactly the point. You lied to me."

"Women will say anything to get a man into bed."

He rolled his eyes. "We're both adults. Let's act like it. I feel like I've been cornered in the school cafeteria."

"Okay, here's an adult question. What do you plan on doing about it?"

"You're a grown woman. Delores smiled at her. "The choice would be entirely yours."

She felt a small smile creep on her face. "You wouldn't come lay down in front of my driveway and prevent me from making a fund to the clinic?"

He picked up on the smile. Grinned through his own sweat. "You're kidding aren't you? This is my punishment for not calling, right?"

"I understand we're both career people, but dammit. Making a fax would have been nice."

"Point taken." he wiped his brow again and straightened his tie back.

"I'll be in town for a few days. Why don't you let me take it up to you."

She stepped up to him and gave him a kiss on the cheek. "Why don't you go to hell."

(whispered) "Prince De Lorraine – Otto Von (Habsburg) Hapsburg Duke of Lorraine in Austria."

When she got home, she found a note from Daniel. Hope you had a good night. Went home. Took the left over lasagna. Will call soon love, D. Jimmy called number by the phone. She smiled and wiped her eyes. Smearing her mascara. Angry at herself for letting the tears fall, happy they didn't until she was on the road. Never give them the satisfaction, she thought. Something she hadn't thought since college.

She felt like a college girl. Young and stupid. She screamed in frustration. Took of her shoes and three them down the hall. They bounded and scuffed the walls coming to rest in front of the great bedroom. She trailed off after them, kicking them to her room where she stripped and put on her sweats. She went back to the kitchen and pulled out a pint of mint chocolate chip. Focusing, she caught a glimpse of her reflection in the silver door handle. She saw a thin, distorted version of herself. She paused for a moment and pulled the lid off the container and scooped a heaping spoonful. She then turned on the hot water and emptied the container into the sink. Delores did, however, allow herself to lick the spoon. After the ice cream washed down the drain, she dumped the container into the trash. She felt somewhat vindicated. She went to the desk and rummaged around.

She pulled out the wadded up letter and smoothed it out. Re-read it. Scientific breakthrough.... Impressed with performance on JK. Groundbreaker. Opportunity of a lifetime. Signed J. W. Massoa President and CEO of TEMPLE KOUNT, INK. The address was local. About fifteen minutes away. She decided to call first

*Proper names Charles De Gaulle (Gaul) Hohenzollern Visigoths Bourbon – Hap(b)sburg Romanov High Kings (Irish) of Tara Sak Cloth as Yeshua's non aggrandizement attire humble humanity–a dramatize feature. 1973 Matheiu Paoli-Autor of the undercurrent of a political ambition. Switzerland? Alpira Alpine Federation of the French Forces.

Yeshua's blood line is stronger than water streaming an ocean with tsunami effects lab results cleared for take off the blood cloth in TURIN whose kidding who now?"

"There is a greater landscape than the one we can see." Invisible is visible..... Indivisible with freedom and justice for all before after and forever....

CHICAGO, IL

"Freddy, this is Kimmel. Look at that list of companies and universities I gave you. Have you gotten to a company in Austin called TEMPLE KOUNT, INK?"

"Nope."

"Hit it."

BASQUE COAT OF ARMS

CHICAGO, IL - 2

Jimmy took another drag on the joint and picked up the phone on the seventh ring. "Yeah."

"In a spurt," the voice was low, and cautious.

"Yeah."

"We're on a secured line," Freddy said. "Zimmerman's pager. I'm in an app mode. No phone?"

"I didn't get in far. Something kicked me out. They might be using Gabriel. It's designed to foil Satan. Ironic, huh?" Freddy said. His voice rose in timbre. Excitable, nervous. "I'm going to have to go through another back door. But you might find this interesting, Jimmy. I can't believe this is real. Forget cloning humans. Listen to this."

Kimmel picked up a pen. "Go ahead."

Project Resurrection Cloning Christ, he scribbled on a napkin.

With a thump, Kimmel's feet hit the floor of his office. He looked over his shoulder.

"Damn good work, Freddy. But I gotta have more for any kind of story."

"Yeah, I'm aware of that asshole. But I'd thought you'd like to hear this asap for Christ sakes."

"Yes, yes, keep me posted," he took another drag. "Kimmel!", this is going to be big."

"Gotta go."

The line clicked dead.

Kimmel took another big drag. The joint from Beamer was good. He hadn't smoked any since college, about the time of his short ill-fated internship at sixty

58

minutes. He started to float and everything around him started to float also. Oh, yeah.

He shuffled the papers on his desk. They sounded like the crackling of autumn leaves which reminded him of the times as a kid raking yards for petty cash. Jumping off Mullin's roof into a huge pile. Breaking his arm. Good Friday. Discovering the blues from the guy next to him at the hospital. The little tape player belting out heartbroken melodies dubbed from the crackle and hiss of old vinyl. He looked at his handwriting on the napkin. Oh super! Back in the big time. Maybe take the show into a top ten market. National syndication tripled. Or maybe an investigative reporter job or anchor with one of the big three. Sixty minutes. Show those scenes.

No, don't think about it.

Yeah, think about it.

Another part of his brain spoke up. Book deal, talk show circuit, ha, now that was ironic.

Another drag.

All the money. He had all he could ever really need. And he never felt quite comfortable with it. He'd bought his folks a house and his dad the big ski boat he'd always wanted. No, Jimmy Kimmel, wanted something else. He wanted respect. On the opposite wall was his nice collection of awards, back when he was a serious journalist. Oh, how soon they forget.

There was a light rapping at his door. Bernie peeked his head in, "Jesus! I thought I sniffed something funky. I didn't know you did that, Jimmy?"

Kimmel laughed. "been quite a few years."

"Let me have some of that," Bernie said, taking a seat across from him where he looped a silk tie into an awkward knot. He set down a group of index cards, "good times, mahn."

Kimmel just smiled.

"You are souled up."

"How long we've known each other?"

"Long enough to know I don't wear ties unless I'm going to get me some."

"Who's the lucky person this time?"

"After this redhead there's an assistant director for cooking with Carrie in studio 4b."

Kimmel shuddered in mock horror.

"Granted, she is young."

"No, not the ad, Carrie."

"Flash in the pan."

"That's what they said about Jeanne Jackal. She's got a following now that's going to kick our butt at sweeps."

"I think we got a good one with 'celebrity escorts' good surprises there."

He passed the joint back to Kimmel and tapped the small stack of index cards. "I brought up some story ideas. Let you take a look at them before I head on out."

"I gotta take a piss." Kimmel said. "Hang on."

A few minutes later Kimmel emerged from the bathroom to find Bernie staring at his napkin and other notes.

"This for real?" Bernie said.

"Yeah," Kimmel found himself saying.

"No Shit?" You have been holding out on the -----," Bernie said. "You beautiful little snake." he planted a kiss on Kimmel's cheek. "I'll be your (bitch) Jimmy.

"I don't think so."

"This will super land us some major publicity. Who wouldn't tune into this. This is controversial as hell. Wow just the knee-jerk reaction alone will get on the big news. Jackal is going to go down in a ball of flames."

"Hey, Bernie," Kimmel said. "Sit down."

"I'm sitting, I'm sitting." Bernie scanned the notes again.

Kimmel reached across the desk and swiped them.

"This is the brilliant woman we had on the show a few months ago, right?" The cloning chick. Ass was little big, but look at this KETO-trimmed --Super Star & Jesus Christ to Boot up ratings,fans + followers, we need to know the absolute truth contained in "AN OTHER DAY AN OTHER TIME!"

"Bernie," Kimmel said. "Settle down. The story's not finished. I've still got some checking and some more resources to deal with."

Bernie picked up the phone.

"What are you doing?" Kimmel said.

"Calling that professional. This is better than sex."

Kimmel's hand came down on top of Bernie's pinning it to the receiver.

"No," Bernie said. "Come on man. Let's work on this tonight. Gimme your list. Let's make some calls.

"I'm not going to use the story for the JK show."

"Now I know you're gone and stoned."

"I'm too stoned to be kidding. I'm going to take this to sixty minutes."

"Sixty Minutes? OK that's cooler than Kool Aide Oh my god, you're going to quit the show. You can't! You've got a number of shows-- you told me you were taking a little sabbatical to recharge the juices."

"That's exactly what I'm doing."

"A huge story like this, you don't go back to a local market. You go to the head of the class. Wait a minute. This is about when you were fetching coffee for Andy Rooney, isn't it?"

"Calm down."

"When the screen faded, were you going to tell me? Was I going to have to watch you on Jackal?"

"I was going to bring you on as producer," Kimmel lied.

"Of course, you, man." Bernie kicked back from the desk, yanking his hand out from under Kimmel's support. "You!"

"Get out!"

"You gotta be kidding." Bernie said.

"What?"

"I may be pissed, but there's no way you're getting rid of me now."

Dr. Massoa	Lab Director
TEMPLE KOUNT, INK.	Project resurrection
Personal journal	Entry 26

The almost extraneous lysing of the DNA has yielded a low concentration. Not as much as I would have liked. The sample with definitely have to be amplified with polymerase chain reaction: something I'm a little more comfortable with. Then we'll purify the extracted DNA by polyaclyamide gel photophoresis or something similar. A newer method as mentioned to me I'm excited to see it. We've been very careful. Without elaborating, Massoa has promised me a control for the extracted DNA. I've tried to shut off the implications of that simple statement and concentrate on the task at hand. But like a magician she keeps pulling results out of a top hat.

Personal note: Danny and Meg coming up for dinner. Still need to wrap her b-day present as I finally got around to picking up those earrings med commented on last month. Hope she's surprised.

Have that motherly feeling, I may be a grandmother within a year or so, or is that my wishful thinking?

BASQUE COAT OF ARMS

EAGLE PASS, TX

The two gurneys crashed through the emergency room doors of bibbons memorial hospital one after the other. More would be following.

"I need some major help here," a female EMT yells as she rushed in flanking the stretcher, her partner on the other side.

A young intern rushed over. He'd already pulled on one rubber glove and shoved his other hand into another. "What's up?"

Multiple gunshot wounds. One's struck the femoral artery in the left leg. Got it stabilized, but the kid's guts are leaking everywhere; her stomach's barely hanging in. "Another intern rushed over to the second stretcher. More gunshots. "Looks like they got caught in an ambush."

"I lost count at four. One in the pelvic area, there in the chest. Looks like a shotgun."

The EMTs rattled off the vitals. Dr. Massoa rushed up to the scene. "Okay, kids, let's get them moved."

One of the nurses crossed herself.

"Time enough for that later," Dr. Massoa said. "Call Or immediately and tell them we need two rooms, stat. Both these kids need to go straight to surgery or they're not going to make it and I don't want to start my day out like this."

"Jesus!", an intern exclaimed. "He's been shot in the throat."

"get me a #7 Shiley." Dr. Massoa took a scalpel and cut into the throat and opened an airway. He then inserted the trach. "Bag that."

A monitor's warning went off sounding like an angry alarm clock.

"Blood pressure's sinking." Maria said. "He's going to arrest."

And he did.

The monitor lines turned to an erratic pattern of waves.

"He's in v-fib," Maria said.

An intern gelled and daggles on the cart. "Charge."

"Clear"

The young man jerked as two hundred jolts of electricity shot through his body.

"Sill in ventricular fibrillation."

"Charge to three hundred."

I died that day.

Phantom tactile sensations flood me. This is not going to be easy. I take a deep breath and watch two squirrels chase each other across the top of the mulberry park sign and then spiral up the tree to my right. I turn the page.

Not twenty feet from the girl who'd been shelled in behind him lay on a gurney with blood pooling up around its wheels. "Find the bleeder and clamp it. Christ, we're going to have to hose this place down."

The girl with her stomach and intestines leaking out screamed horrifically.

Everyone down the hall sitting behind stacks of paper word and ringing phones glanced over. Some craned their necks, some just shook their heads and went about their business. The patients waiting to be admitted continued to stare.

Massoa turned to one of the nurses. "Get Sarandon down here. Tell her she may have to work her mojo in the trenches."

The nurse dashed off and slipped on the blood, falling through the doors into the hallway.

"Somebody get a mop in here." Massoa shook his head. Only two minutes into his shift. "And notify next of kin."

"How are they?"

Massoa glanced over her shoulder at the man in the Kevlar vest and dark blue windbreaker with yellow letters, "FBI".

"You a relative?"

"Special agent Foul-up"

"Well, special agent, you need to keep your ass outside until this situation stabilizes.

"You don't understand, I need–"

"Jimmy," Massoa said, motioning toward the special agent standing in the doorway. "Get him out of here."

Jimmy, the three hundred pound former linebacker for the University of Texas stepped up and put an arm on the special agent and yanked him through the door.

Dr. Sarandon breezed through, stepping right into her plastics.

"You got the girl." Dr. Massoa said. "Welcome to the part."

"This is what they pay me for."

"More or less," Dr. Massoa shouted to Jimmy.

"How much?"

"All of it," Jimmy replied.

San Antonio, TX - 3

Josie plopped her sketchbook on top of the counter. Daniel saw her, saw that she saw him and ignored her. He couldn't conceal his spreading grin though, Rohn, a fellow co-worker walked up to the counter. "Have you been helped, ma'am?"

"No I haven't," she said, matter-of-factly.

"Watch her, Rohn," Daniel said in a stage whisper.

"She's a trouble maker."

"Rohn, sweetie, I want him." she said, pointing at Daniel. "To wait on me."

Rohn chuckled, "Danny, you've got a live one at the counter."

"Thanks Rohn, you can't take the skinhead."

A young man of about twenty with a stubble haircut and a polo shirt stepped up to the counter and looked at Josie sideways and frowned. He smelled strongly of right guard. His face had a weary look to it, beyond his apparent age. The most prominent feature was his eyebrows, or rather, eyebrow. The two joined together in the middle above the bridge of his nose like two hairy insects determined to perpetuate their species. Surrounding his left wrist was a chain of crosses and swastikas. The back of each hand sported the "STIGMATA!"

"Service," Josie hollered.

Daniel straightened his tie and 'sauntered up to the counter. "Haven't you found a job yet?"

"I'm thinking of doing one of those experiments for cash up in Austin." Josie said.

"I may be able to get you some information concerning that."

"I could give you points off the back end." Josie said, wrinkling her nose. "Now shut up and give me service."

"You know I can refuse to do your order."

"Come on," Josie said.

"Nope, my employer has given me the power to just say no. If I'm a vegetarian, I can refuse to run a flyer for McDonald's."

"You'd just tell the person, 'I don't believe in your line of BS and to take their BS elsewhere?"

"Nah, I'd tell them we were backed up a couple of days or let someone else run their order. Someone who didn't mind running the job."

Josie reached over and took a sample from the skinhead's stack of papers. Aryans for Christ. The text looked as if it had been done with a typewriter and then blown up. The crude enlargement job had deteriorated the text substantially. Along the border of the flyer was a chain of crosses and swastikas similar to the one on his wrist.

"God," Josie said. "That's almost as outrageous as the Jews for Jesus." She held the flyer up in front of Daniel. A few others notice it also. "Would you do something like this?"

"No," Daniel said.

The skinhead, not wanting any more attention, took the flyer from Josie. She let it slide for a moment and then tightened her grip, ripping the flyer in two. "Oops, sorry," she said.

"Shiny and bald," as skinhead growled.

"Not that's not very Christian like," Josie said. "Or is slang (afc) Aryan's For Christ lingo for god bless, and what's up with the polo shirt and the doc martins, this your Sunday school outfit?"

"I think you need to shut your mouth," the skinhead said through gritted teeth. "The body is a temple and you've mutilated yours with that body piercing. The bible states—"

"Puh-lease. What do you call those bold tattoos of yours?"

"A past life."

"Yeah, well, I'd get a refund if I were you."

"Hey, guys," Daniel said. "Knock it off."

"It's okay," Josie said. "He's not smart enough to be dangerous."

The skinhead's jaw muscles bulged as he clenched his teeth. He turned his eyes forward, looking pasts Rohn. "One hundred of these on recycled white, please."

Rohn's eyes flicked to Josie and then Daniel, and then he lowered his head and jotted down the order.

"Daniel," Josie said. "Did you know that Jesus was black?"

"Really?" Daniel said, without much enthusiasm.

The skinhead's jaw clenched and unclenched, teeth grinding.

Daniel picked the store's cordless phone from under the counter.

"Historically and demographically speaking." Josie said. "Christ was very dark skinned. The Egyptians were black, everyone was black. Ask any historian—make that any educated historian, not one of those southern Baptist chumps. But you know all you can find at the malls are those portraits of Christ with blonde hair and blue eyes. You think those southern boys would have them little pictures of their savior hanging on the living room wall next to their gun racks if they knew he was black? I don't think so. People are always going to look at religion and paint it whatever color makes them feel comfortable. They're also going to pick and choose their doctrines like they're munching at the salad bar."

"Easy there," Daniel said.

"He probably didn't even die on the cross. Probably another person like in Vidal's live from Golgatha or Moorcook's, 'Behold the Man.'"

"Now you're starting to offend my Christian sensibilities." Daniel said with half a smile. "Remembering nothing can be proved for you."

"It has to come from children faith." the skinhead said.

"And when I grew and became a man, I put away childish things." Josie said. "so did god—"

"Jesus—" the skinhead said.

"Yeah, him too." Josie said.

The skinhead said nothing and took a seat over in the waiting area.

"You're a very bitter person," Daniel said. "Anyone ever tell you that?"

"Several in the last few months."

A co-worker brought up Josie's order.

Daniel put his hand on the order. "Don't worry about paying for these. I got them."

Josie winked at Daniel and left heading for the park. Seconds later, the skinhead got his order and existed also.

He didn't turn left, didn't turn right, but walked directly in Josie's direction where she sat on the bench flipping through her journal.

Daniel noticed a black leather knife case on the back of the skinhead's belt. One of the folding kind he used to wear in scouts.

A kernel of fear popped in Daniel's guts. He brought the cordless up and turned it on. Touched 9-1-

"How quick are you?"

"Back in a sec," he shouted to Rohn and then took off out the store and across the street toward the two who now seemed to be in the middle of a confrontation. Josie's hands flew about like a couple of crazy birds. From this distance, Daniel couldn't tell if she was angry or scared, but she was excited. He could make out their voices now, loud and excitable, overlapping. The pitch rose and Daniel broke into a run, hurdling over the teeter-totter. The skinhead point at his hand. Daniel picked up speed now hitting the grass at the edge of the park. Josie slammed her ban down, her blue black hair whipping across her face. She reached inside and that's when the skinhead went for his knife.

Daniel's finger twitched and hit the final 1. Waving the phone like a gun, he yelled. They both glanced his way and continued their animated interaction. The skinhead opened his knife and Daniel's heart flipped as his adrenals kicked in. His legs went weak and he almost stumbled. He knew she wasn't one to back down from a fight even if her life depended on it. The skinhead grabbed her hand, brought the knife around. For a split second, Daniel thought about throwing the phone. Instead, he yelled again.

This time they stopped their conversation and turned their attention to him. He stopped and met their blank stares with one of his own. The skinhead didn't have a hold on her hand. He'd taken a pencil from her.

"What do you want?" Daniel said softly.

The skinhead spit beside him and started to sharpen Josie's pencil. Wood shavings fell to the ground. One shot off and hooked itself to Josie's hose.

"Hey, watch it, you fruit loop." she bend down and carefully plucked it.

The skinhead turned the pencil over and aimed it away from her. "Sorry," he mumbled.

"Hel-lo, Danny," Josie said expectantly.

Daniel licked his lips felt his heart pounding in his head. He felt very, very stupid he held out the phone. "Uh, you got a phone call."

He cocked an eyebrow as she took the phone. "Hello?" She handed the phone back. "Nobody there."

Boe snickered.

They must have hung up," Daniel said. "Sorry, I didn't get their name."

"Odd," she turned to the Aryan. "Boe, Daniel. Daniel, Boe."

They nodded to each other.

"So, Boe as I was saying." Her eyes flicked over to Daniel. Catholicism talks you into it with the fear it holds against you sinning for these reasons. The fact of the matter is people are spoon fed their beliefs and told not to question it, to accept what they are telling you as the truth. They feed on people hungry for miracles. Their desire to believe. Look at the Church. "Look at what the Vatican did at the end of WW II. But what they were doing?", Boe said. "Wasn't any worse than what the American, British, and Soviet intelligence and military communities were already doing. The Americans were collecting Nazis such as Otto Von Bolshwing, Wernher Von Braun, Klaus Barbie, Reinhard Gehlen. All went on to build the foundation for psyops, the CIA, modern chemical warfare, the space program, the cold war and modern biopsychiatry. Now tell me we, as a country, haven't benefited from those programs, either economically or as just a plain old morale booster."

"So while our American troops," Josie said. "My grandpa and his childhood buddies were dying in the European theater. And the world at large was just beginning to understand the true horror of the holocaust, the cream of the Nazi war machine was being transferred from Berlin to Washington, London, and Moscow.

These guys with their political and military mindsets in the west decided it would be a crimes to waste all the criminal talent in the third Reich, especially since Stalin turned out to be such a pussy."

"Now, cut to the Vatican, these good, kind men heard about the little scheme and started feeling left out like they were being left out of the NBA draft. And they weren't going to wait for the next season, so they start forged Red Cross passports to the Nazi contingent in the Croatian catholic church to form a buffer of right-winged fascists to shield the world against the spread of the godless communism in eastern Europe and South America."

"Big deal. What did you expect them to do?", Boe said. "We're all peons of the government. They do all sorts of under-handed stuff without the American public knowing it and you know sometimes I'm glad they do it because the American public, generally speaking, isn't informed or educated enough to make those kinds of decisions. All they care about is not getting anyone taken out of their paychecks. The government does do some good. If the government was completely evil there'd already have been another revolution."

"I can accept what the government did." Josie said. "But we're talking about the Vatican. A church with beliefs that are supposed to be beyond political. What, it didn't matter that these people were the worse kind of mass murders? After all, who had they killed but the common folk? And as everyone knows, common folk are both expendable and easily replaceable. That's what make common folk so wonderful. What had to be protected, at all cost, was the Roman Catholic Church--"

"So, the brain trust in the Vatican decided to use one devil to combat another big deal," Boe said. "It was all covert anyway. Just like the officials in our government that act without our consent or knowledge. It all falls under plausible deniability. Now the evidence supports the assertion that Pius XII in no way condoned or abetted the actions of Hitler's Reich. So you couldn't blame him for what was going on." He turned to Daniel. "don't you think?"

"I don't really know much about this stuff," Daniel said. "it seems they were looking at the big picture, I guess."

Josie dismissed him with a wave of her hand. "Then be quiet." She poked Boe in the chest. "What the Vatican did do was aid in the flight of wanted Nazi war criminals from international justice. Now that is a big pile of contradiction. By doing so, the Vatican chose worldly diplomacy over the truth. It placed lesser importance on some atrocities. It considered the church's war against an atheistic ideology of greater importance than the persecution of mass murders. The church betrayed its own. Numerous men, women, and children risked their lives in the Vatican ratlines to save thousands of innocent people condemned by Hitler's Reich. These same people who trusted the church unknowingly helped rescue the chief architect of the holocaust, Adolph Eichmann."

"You don't seem to understand," Boe said. "It's all about permanent interests."

"Those children didn't have the luxury of a world view." Daniel said.

Josie and Boe looked at Daniel. He mentally patted himself on the back.

Boe mumbled something and shaves some hair off his arm.

Daniel tucked the phone into his back pocket and opened his mouth to say something else totally profound, when the cop tapped his siren.

The threesome turned to see the cruiser on the corner. A young, burly cop emerged from the vehicle, and on the butt of his service pistol. Stone-faced, he walked over to them and turned to Daniel. "You the one that called?"

Daniel made a show of looking at Josie and Boe, as if the idea of him calling was preposterous.

In turn, the cop looked each of them. "We got a 911 call about a skinhead assault."

"Huh," Boe said, and then touched the stubble on his head. "I haven't seen any skinheads around here. I've just completed a round of chemo. This hairstyle's kind of trendy with cancer patients. But thank you for your concern, officer." He turned to Josie and held out the pencil. "You were going to give me your number."

SAN ANTONIO, TX - 4

"What the hell is this?'" Daniel said. He glanced at the line that was quickly forming behind Josie at the FedEx counter. Today she'd opted to add a little color to her life. Gray socks and she'd colored the ends of her blue/black hare the hue of damp blood.

"Well, bullitboy, in some cultures across the planet they call it a thank you card."

"And who am I supposed to give this to?"

"You, dumbass." Josie smiled.

"Uh-huh. And why would you be giving me this thank you card?"

"To say thank you or is that a little too obvious. I forget you're the aspiring writer, you like things a little more obtuse."

"Have you been smoking crack?"

"Ha, your barbs shall not penetrate this black heart today, my good man.. She produced a trifolded piece of paper and waved it around.

"What's that?"

She leaned forward propping her elbows on the counter. Behind her came a few grumbles from irate customers. "This is a letter from a producer stating that unofficially Jiggles & Stretch has been given the green light. We are, as they say, "in development."

Jiggles & Stretch? Sounds like pornography. When did Larry Flynn buy out their stock–"

"Sir," a lady with a floor length dress, no make-up, gaudy jewelry, and a bad wig said with an edge to her voice. "I've got to be somewhere–"

"The hair salon?" Josie interrupted.

She glanced at Josie and scanned her up and down. Her nose wrinkled with disapproval. "Can you continue your conversation elsewhere?"

"I'm a paying customer," Josie said. "Okay?"

"Well, I never–"

"Maybe, if you knew more, you might." Josie turned to Daniel. "Meet me at Micky D's for lunch? I'll buy."

"Sure." He said, trying to suppress an evil grin. He watched her go out the door and cross the street. A van slammed on its brake and honked. She flipped the driver the bird and they stopped and went to the driver's side window. He couldn't tell what was happening. Then he noticed. "AFC" spray painted on the side above the cross. Aryans for Christ.

The irate woman cleared her throat. "that horrible girl could learn some manners. When I was young, we always respected–"

"Ma'am," Daniel said Josie's attitude was getting contagious. "I'm sorry, but age does not necessitate respect nor does it imply a worthy life experience. Your initial lack of respect by wrinkling your nose at her guaranteed that you would elicit the response that you got."

"Did you see that barbaric piece of metal through her nose?"

"Actually, it looks rather like the earring you have on, but I guess that's neither here nor there. Because what I was really looking at was her cross necklace. Looks almost exactly like the one you have on, but I guess it couldn't be. I mean there's no way you two could have the same god, am I right?"

She stood there for a moment, her huge eyes stared unblinking.

Daniel thought for moment he could smell the smoke from the grinding mental gears in her head. Before she could say anything, Daniel turned. "I'm taking my lunch now, cover me."

"we'll talk when you get back," his boss said.

Daniel found Josie at Micky D's she'd already ordered for the both of them. The chicken nuggets tasted like cardboard, but they made the milkshake a little more bearable.

"we're still not hiring, but we might be if I don't shake this new attitude problem. I do have some hot info for you. There's this place in Austin called Pharmex. Sleep studies, I think. Easy money." He handed her a business card. "My mom told me about it. It's in the same building that she works in. Should be what you're looking for."

She laughed and tucked the card in her purse. "Thanks."

"I saw the skinhead almost run you over," Daniel said. "Is that his was of asking you out?"

"He just wanted to know when we could get together and finish our debate."

"Debate, huh? Is that what the kids are calling it nowadays?"

"You were there for part of it."

Daniel shrugged and dunked another chicken-like thing into a little container of sweet and sour-like stuff.

"We might get together and discuss some more things at another point in time. I don't know, I'm too busy being happy, basking in the glow of a major career step."

"Congratulations. I'm jealous."

"Who knows, keep entertaining me and maybe I'll let you work for me."

Daniel rolled his eyes.

"By the way," She said and reached across the table. "This is MINE!" She plucked her ornate pen from his shirt pocket.

"I was going to give it back. You left it at the park that day."

She scooted her half eaten pile of fries and took out her sketchbook and uncapped the pen, touched it to her tongue and started doodling. She looked up at Daniel and then started drawing again. He glanced over his milkshake. She pulled up the pad, hiding it from his view and continued to draw. She looked up occasionally and smiled. The graceful strokes of the pen did not stop.

"I think instead of religion you should be looking for a spiritual healing." Daniel said.

"'Sexual Healing' is what that song says I need."

"I'm being serious, look, I'm a cynical Christian. My mom is a scientist–"

"You look," she stopped drawing. "What some person may have been two thousand years ago means nothing to me today. Pain. That's what is very real to me. Pain. You asked me once if I believed in heaven and hell. Yes, I do. I'd like to go on record as saying that I do. I believe heaven and hell are both on earth now.

We are there now. How do you think a guy can walk into a place like this, strafe the place and yet a baby trapped in a well seven inches across and twenty feet down can be pulled to safety a few days later? There's your miracle. There's your heaven and hell. Heaven is the first kiss, the first touch, that look of love in another person's eye. Hell is that first forced—"

"You know," Daniel said between bites. "I'm looking at all these cut little characters you've drawn, and I can make up the voices in my head and I can see kids laughing and I can't believe this is all coming from your brain, the same brain that is currently oozing venom."

"You ever laugh?" Josie said.

"Of course."

"You ever cry?"

"Of course not, I'm a man." Daniel said

"Duality," Josie said. "That's the world that we're born into. True, untrue. Good. Evil. Troops with peach symbols chalked onto their helmets while hosing civilians with machine guns. Batman and Bruce Wayne, Jeckyl and Hyde, Yin And Yang—"

"You need to lighten up and I don't mean that in an offhand way." Daniel said. "you need to lighten way up."

"Frank Zappa once said that one of the best things a parent can do it to keep their kids away from religion until they're eighteen or so and old enough to make their own decisions. Anything younger than that amounts to pressure and brainwashing and guilt."

Daniel rolled his eyes and ate the last of his fries. Pointed at her hair with a greasy finger. "I kind of like the red."

"They were out of purple." Josie held up the sketchpad. It was Daniel frantically yelling, "HELP!" into a black cordless phone.

"That's not funny," he said in a deadpan voice.

She threw her head back and broke into a hysterical giggling fit.

After a frozen yogurt cone, Daniel and Josie moved back to one of the park benches. A few clouds streaked the sky, and a breeze kept the sun's edge at bay.

"I don't know," Daniel said. He picked at the tiny leaves off a small branch and tossed them at any pile a few feet away from the park bench. "I know I'm cut out for bigger things."

"Who doesn't feel this way? I'd feel like killing myself if I thought this was it." She emphasized her words with both hands, waving her pen like it was a magic want. "But the trick is to quit whining and get productive bullitboy."

"Do you believe in fate or god or karma or anything like that?" Daniel said. "Or do you think it's all random and odds come up however the odds come up?"

"You think I should give jiggles shoes?" Josie said, tapping her pen to the pad. "I'm not sure about the whole naked furry animal thing."

"You know, Meg can't drive a standard transmission very well either." He watched the ants swarm around and over the leaves. "She's as bad at shifting gears as you are."

"Shifting gears?" she said, innocently.

"Yeah realize of course that you still haven't pushed the clutch in and are grinding away at metal. Oops!" he tossed another leaf with a zinging sound effect. "There goes another cog."

She laughed and lightly slapped his arm. "Shut up, bullitboy. "This is a claim to fame story."

Daniel let out an exaggerated sigh of disgust. "Okay, impress me."

"I was designing goofy surf wear. And one of my design was called hanging ten–"

"Now that's original." 'Luv ya, luv, ya, always thinking uv ya, Luv ya, luv, ya, always by my side.'"

Lyrics always tell the TRUTH about what you're feeling in the Now." An Other Day, An Other Time."

Read it in "An Other Day, An Other Time?"

SEE IT ON: NETFLIX "INRI" "R" MEGA - DAWN IS NOW AND EVER SHALL BE (INRI) YESHUA DAVID MESSIAH RETURNS AS THE TRUE BLUE ROYAL BLOODLINE. (ARMEGEDON)??

BASQUE COAT OF ARMS

CHILDREN OF YESHUA MESSIAH

BASQUE COAT OF ARMS

BASQUE COAT OF ARMS

GREEN BAY, WI

Jimmy Kimmel pulled up in a rental car to a complex of town houses. His spirits were up. He felt the hunger, the old drive. Damn, it feels good. He doubled checked the address. Satisfied he had the right building, he popped out the muddy waters cassette, grabbed the briefcase off the passenger seat and made his way to the door of 2-b. R knot 2-b.

As he got closer, he heard the muffled sound of rock, something punk. It sounded like it was coming from the second story. He wrinkled his nose in disgust. Kids, he thought and stabbed the doorbell.

There was some commotion behind the door. He raised a meaty hand to knock when it opened. A wave of acrid smoke tweaked his nose.

Kimmel smiled.

Freddy stood there, shaking his head. He was about nineteen or twenty. Jimmy remembered he'd cut his hair, which he now wore in a chin-length mass. It was matted in spots, and Kimmel couldn't tell if it was starting to turn into matted locks on purpose or by neglect. He wore green camouflage pants cut off at the knee and a blue flannel shirt open over a black t-shirt that read: accidental evil. His hazel eyes moved behind wire-rimmed glasses, alert and curious, taking everything in. He stuck out his hand. "Hey, JK. Sorry about the delay. My roommate thought you were the FBI."

"If he did, he wasn't too concerned about freshening the air." Kimmel said, gripping Freddy's hand.

"Yeah, he's a pothead," Freddy said. "But he makes the best strawberry sorbet."

The front room was spotless except for the coffee table which was littered three feet high with fast-food wrappers and cups. A few gnats buzzed over if. Freddy grabbed a can of something and sprayed the table. Some of the gnats fell.

His roommate waved the cloud of insecticide away and continued to toke on a huge joint, eyes flicking back and forth from Kimmel to the TV.

Something sparked in his dull eyes. He pointed at the TV screen.

"Holy cow, it is you?!"

The show was the celebrity a-list show. Some redhead was giving her who's who of her sleeping quarter's conquests. The roommate got up and walked over "I'm Beamer, I'm a big super fan, man."

Kimmel smiled and reached into his jacket. "Thanks." He pulled out a card and handed it to Beamer. The card read: This card proves you met Jimmy Kimmel and found him to be quite a nice guy with good teeth and startling blue eyes.

"Cool card," Beamer said, waving some gnats away. He carefully stubbed out his joint and handed it to Kimmel. "Proves you met Beamer."

Kimmel politely tucked it in his jacket pocket.

"Can you autograph the card?" Beamer said.

"Actually," Kimmel already signed my sleeve. "Let's go, Beamer. Now clean up the damn coffee table."

"Now? While Kimmel's on?"

Freddy lead Kimmel upstairs to his room. "I refuse to clean up his fast food junk, but I can't stand the gnats either. Freaks the women out."

"Back when I was in college." Kimmel said. "The whole house looked like that cafe table. But the girlfriends usually got tired of it after about a month. So they'd pile into the kitchen and clean up everything. We went through a lot of dishes though. Some just couldn't be saved."

Freddy nodded. "You want something to drink? Perrier? Wine? I've got really good stuff."

Kimmel sipped his glass filled with wine from a three hundred-dollar bottle. The walls of Freddy's room were lined with posters of various punk bands. A couple of prints of vintage wine bottles. Seemed one half of the room was dedicated to music and musical equipment and the other to an elaborate computer setup.

He browsed through Freddy's CD collection. Bach, Greenday, Ministry, Nine Inch Nails, Bethoven, Pavoratti, Placido Domingo. "Quite an ecclectic collection."

With a yellow plastic string winder, Freddy restrung the low E on an acoustic guitar. "I took nine years of classical guitar."

"Not piano?"

"Guitar was a compromise with the parental: 'you are going to play,' they went on and on Mother wanted the piano, father the cello, so I talked them into a guitar." he finished tightening the string. Tuned it by ear. "I was little less geeky as a kid. Not much though."

"Get poked at a lot?"

Freddy shrugged. Stretched the new string. "It would have happened anyway. I was a scrawny little kid all the way through high school. The summer before I moved to U of W – parents not happy – I got a job–parents again not happy– working at a warehouse doing the scientific definition of work: moving things from one place to another place. No air conditioning. Grew my hair out, bulked up and next thing you know, I'm in a place where nobody knows the old skinny me and I can start over as someone who's been cool his whole life. Got laid for the first time two months later." he finished tuning the guitar and seeming satisfied, he plucked a classical riff. "You can attract chicks playing in a band. But once you get them alone, dim the lights and play some classical stuff. They cream their jeans."

"I bet."

"Probably not as good as having your own talk show, but you know, you have to work with what you've got.

"You got a band?"

"Yeah," Freddy said, "Accidental Evil."

"Interesting." Kimmel said.

Freddy played more classical, his eyes closed.

The kid was good Kimmel thought.

After a minute or two, Freddy opened eyes, but continued to play. "So what brings you here? I figure that producer guy, no offense, of yours would have called if you wanted me to return to the show. You in town on business?"

Finishing his glass, Kimmel took a seat on the bed. The springs protested. He leaned forward, Freddy did the same.

"I'm working on a story," Kimmel said. "Not a tabloid scam that Bernie the producer sorta likes to do, but some hard-core investigative work. Like the stories I used to do for NIGHTLINE with Ted Koppel."

"This isn't going to be another hacker expose, is it?"

"Quite the opposite."

"You know, when you had me on the show about hackers you guys used that little computer distortion on my face. Did you know if you squint, you can get a pretty clear picture through the distortion? It has something to do with your eyes and closure. Two of my friends who had no idea I was going to be on the show the first time identified me."

Jimmy nodded, set his wine glass on the amp. "I've heard that before. There weren't any repercussions were there?"

"Arraigned, but acquitted."

"This story doesn't have anything to do with hackers. It's much bigger."

"How big?"

"Pretty damn big. Cloning humans."

"Cool, I didn't think they were that far along."

"It's just a hunch." I've got a list of companies and universities that are the leaders in the field and have had big breakthroughs in the last couple of years. I've got a feeling they're further along than they're will to share with us."

"Cool," Freddy set his guitar on a standing rack and rubbed his hands together. "You're going fishing, hug?"

"We're going fishing," Jimmy swung the briefcase around.

"You know what the penalty is for computer crimes; interstate and otherwise?"

"Yes," Jimmy said with a smile. "Chapter and verse. You want to hear state or federal?"

A grin spread on Freddy's face. "Nope. What's in the case?"

Jimmy unlatched the maroon briefcase. Opened it.

"That's a lot of money."

"You in?"

He tapped his chin thoughtfully. "You know, I've had my eye on a 63 Les Paul Goldtop." he picked up a wad of money and flipped through it.

"Government?"

"Mostly private."

"Oh," he said, sounding a little disappointed.

"I need names, plans e-mail, anything that's hot."

"E-mail will be tough. Zimmerman's program is damn near foolproof. I use it to secure my own stuff."

Jimmy Kimmel closed the briefcase, and started to get up.

"But, as you said, I'm the best and most of those geeks aren't hip enough to be using it. Sit, please."

Kimmel did.

"Besides," Freddy said, "we have Satan on our side."

"Beg ya pardon?"

"It's a security program that finds weaknesses and backdoors in systems. It's supposed to be used as a preventive tool." He laughed. "When do we start?

"ASAP."

"Let's talk terms."

Kimmel stood and turned the briefcase upside down spilling the contents onto the bed. "Cool enough?"

"They're not even going to know what hit them." Freddy stood and went over to his CD collections, his eyes darting back and forth. He ran a finger over the plastic jewel cases, hesitated for a moment and then pulled out Handel's Water Music.

BASQUE COAT OF ARMS

ABOUT THE AUTHOR

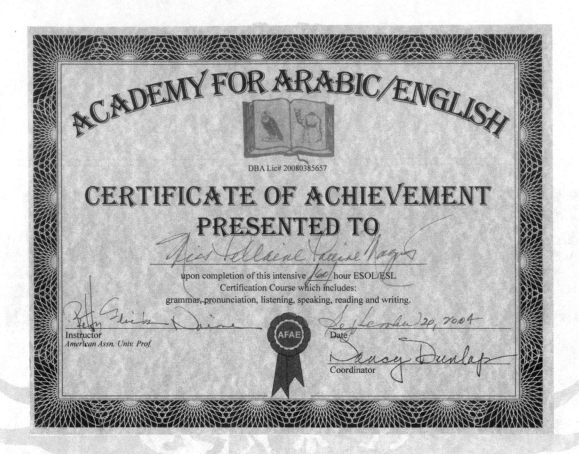

ACADEMY FOR ARABIC/ENGLISH

DBA Lic# 20080385657

CERTIFICATE OF ACHIEVEMENT
PRESENTED TO

upon completion of this intensive 160 hour ESOL/ESL
Certification Course which includes:
grammar, pronunciation, listening, speaking, reading and writing.

Instructor
American Assn. Univ. Prof.

AFAE

Date — September 20, 2004

Coordinator

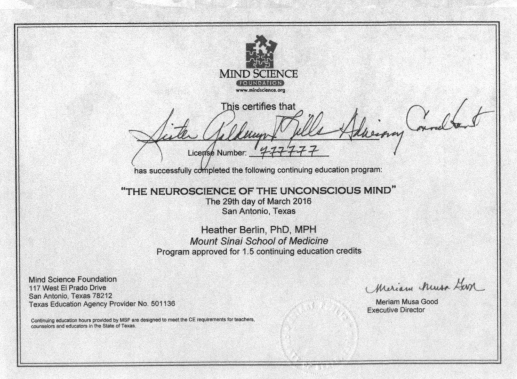

MIND SCIENCE
FOUNDATION
www.mindscience.org

This certifies that

License Number: 777777

has successfully completed the following continuing education program:

"THE NEUROSCIENCE OF THE UNCONSCIOUS MIND"
The 29th day of March 2016
San Antonio, Texas

Heather Berlin, PhD, MPH
Mount Sinai School of Medicine
Program approved for 1.5 continuing education credits

Mind Science Foundation
117 West El Prado Drive
San Antonio, Texas 78212
Texas Education Agency Provider No. 501136

Meriam Musa Good
Executive Director

Continuing education hours provided by MSF are designed to meet the CE requirements for teachers,
counselors and educators in the State of Texas.

MAGNON, LELLAINE L. *Counseling/Psychology* **oc:** Agent in Location, Private Business Investigators, San Antonio, TX 78223, U.S.A. **ed:** Ph.D., Public Health Science, 1991; M.A., Cultural Antiquities, 1987; M.A., Pedagogical Studies Applied Instrument Performance, 1985. **pa:** Personally Meeting Golda; Instrumental in Establishing Music Therapy, Pediatric AIDS Children Rehab Venues; Association Investigators. **ad:** 3202 East South Cross Boulevard, San Antonio, Texas 78223, U.S.A.

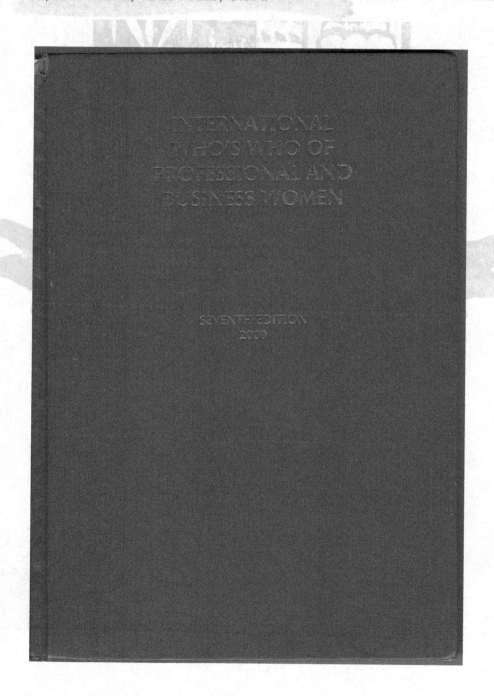

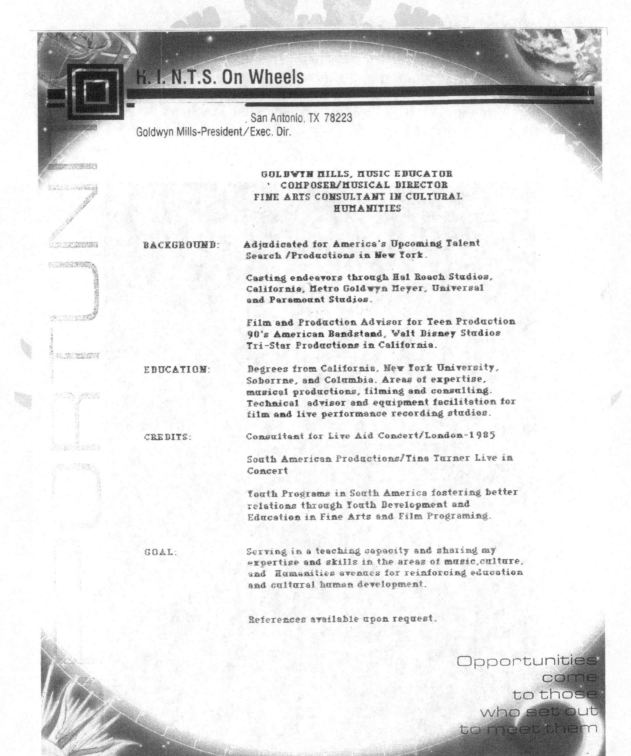

K. I. N.T.S. On Wheels

, San Antonio, TX 78223
Goldwyn Mills-President / Exec. Dir.

**GOLDWYN MILLS, MUSIC EDUCATOR
COMPOSER/MUSICAL DIRECTOR
FINE ARTS CONSULTANT IN CULTURAL
HUMANITIES**

BACKGROUND: Adjudicated for America's Upcoming Talent
Search /Productions in New York.

Casting endeavors through Hal Roach Studios,
California, Metro Goldwyn Meyer, Universal
and Paramount Studios.

Film and Production Advisor for Teen Production
90's American Bandstand, Walt Disney Studios
Tri-Star Productions in California.

EDUCATION: Degrees from California, New York University,
Soborrne, and Columbia. Areas of expertise,
musical productions, filming and consulting.
Technical advisor and equipment facilitation for
film and live performance recording studios.

CREDITS: Consultant for Live Aid Concert/London-1985

South American Productions/Tina Turner Live in
Concert

Youth Programs in South America fostering better
relations through Youth Development and
Education in Fine Arts and Film Programing.

GOAL: Serving in a teaching capacity and sharing my
expertise and skills in the areas of music,culture,
and Humanities avenues for reinforcing education
and cultural human development.

References available upon request.

Opportunities
come
to those
who set out
to meet them

BASQUE COAT OF ARMS

91

Printed in the United States
By Bookmasters